D1287389

The Teacher's Guide to the Four-Blocks®
Literacy Model

Grade 2

A Multimethod,
Multilevel Literacy
Framework

Guided Reading

Self-Selected Reading

Writing

Working with Words

by
Patricia M. Cunningham
Dorothy P. Hall
Cheryl M. Sigmon

Carson-Dellosa Publishing, Inc.
Greensboro, North Carolina

ISBN 978-1-604180-74-9

Table of Contents

OVERVIEW

INTRODUCTION TO THE FOUR BLOCKS

Welcome to Second Grade

When elementary teachers are asked which grade they would like to teach, more teachers choose second grade than any other grade! Why do so many elementary teachers want to teach second grade? Most second-grade teachers will tell you that second graders are still cute and huggable—but they know how to do the many things that schools want them to know how to do. Most second graders love school—and their teachers—and are eager to learn whatever we teach them.

Teaching reading and writing to second graders is challenging yet rewarding. The challenge is that students come to second grade at a variety of reading levels. Some students are reading and writing exceptionally well, and second-grade teachers feel responsible for continuing their accelerated growth and making sure that they remain eager and motivated readers and writers. Some second graders come to second grade reading and writing at exactly the level we expect from beginning second graders, and we want to be sure that they continue to grow as they encounter the more complex second-grade materials and skills.

However, some second graders struggle with reading and writing. Those are students about whom we worry. The struggling readers and writers know some words and have some decoding and comprehension strategies, but often they have trouble applying their strategies as they read and write. They lack fluency in both reading and writing, and they approach literacy activities reluctantly and without much confidence. Sometimes, when students struggle with reading and writing in kindergarten and first grade, they decide that reading and writing are activities at which they are not good. These students have already given up thinking that they can become good readers and writers and, consequently, don't put forth much effort. Teachers of struggling readers in second grade must structure their reading instruction so that these struggling readers experience some success and begin to believe that they will become good readers and writers this year.

In addition to coming to second grade at different literacy levels, second graders come with their own personalities. The best approach to literacy for one student will often not be the best approach for another student. Four Blocks was developed to incorporate four different methods of teaching reading so that all students have some instruction in the method through which they learn best. In Four-Blocks classrooms, students participate daily in Guided Reading, Self-Selected Reading, Writing, and Working with Words activities. As teachers engage students in these four different blocks, they make their instruction multilevel so that students at all literacy levels can learn from the activities and move forward.

This teacher's guide will help you get started using the Four-Blocks framework in your second-grade classroom. Filled with practical ideas and examples, it will help you use your favorite ideas, books, and materials in the most effective ways possible. Four Blocks has some guidelines, but it is not a prescriptive program. You, the second-grade teacher, know your students best, and you want them to achieve. Our hope is that the activities and suggestions in this guide will help you make this the best second-grade year ever for you and your students.

Pat Cunningham and Dottie Hall

What Is the History of Four Blocks?

Four Blocks is a framework for reading and writing that includes all of the components of a comprehensive instructional program. The framework was developed in a first-grade classroom in Winston-Salem, North Carolina, during the 1989–1990 school year. The teachers who conducted the first investigation wanted to develop a model of first-grade instruction that took into account students' various learning styles and personal preferences. The teachers wanted to be sure that the instructional model met the diverse needs of a heterogeneous class of first graders.

Over the last century, there have been four major approaches to beginning reading instruction. The basal approach emphasizes gradually increasing levels of difficulty and teacher-guided reading of short selections. Phonics instruction places the main emphasis on learning letter-sound relationships. A third approach focuses on individualized reading; students choose what they want to read, and teachers give them help. The fourth major approach is writing-based, in which the first material students read is generally their own writing and that of their classmates. Each approach has its benefits, and different approaches are effective for different students.

Over the course of the school year, first graders in the investigational classroom learned through an integrated program that combined all four approaches: Guided Reading, Self-Selected Reading, Writing, and Working with Words. When tested at year's end, students showed significant progress. In fact, one student who would probably have been put in the lowest-ability group at the beginning of the year was reading at the fourth-grade level (Cunningham, Hall, and Defee 1991).

Since that first classroom, Four Blocks has spread around the United States and into Canada. Although most often applied in grades one, two, and three, Four Blocks can also be used in kindergarten (as Building Blocks) and the upper grades (as Big Blocks).

The Four-Blocks framework for reading and writing was developed by teachers who believed that to be successful in teaching all students to read and write, we have to do it all! "Doing it all" means incorporating on a daily basis the different approaches to reading. By doing all of the four blocks each day, teachers acknowledge that students do not all learn in the same way. They can provide substantial instruction to support the various learning personalities of students in their classrooms.

Next, you will learn more about how the Four-Blocks framework can help you and your students succeed.

What Is Four Blocks?

	GUIDED READING
Goals	■ To teach comprehension skills and strategies ■ To develop students' background knowledge, meaningful vocabulary, and oral language ■ To teach students how to read all types of literature ■ To provide as much instructional-level reading as possible ■ To maintain the motivation and self-confidence of struggling readers
Before Reading	■ The teacher introduces and supports text with the whole group of students to prepare them to read the chosen text. ■ Before-reading preparation may include activating and building prior knowledge, introducing and discussing key vocabulary, modeling a think-aloud, starting a graphic organizer or KWL chart, starting a story map, previewing and making predictions, setting a clear purpose for reading, or focusing on a particular comprehension strategy.
During Reading	■ The teacher provides reading support for students using flexible grouping formats. ■ Grouping may include pairs, whole group, Playschool Groups or Reading Teams, Three-Ring Circus, or Book Clubs/Literature Circles.
After Reading	■ Whatever purpose was set for reading is immediately followed up after reading. ■ Activities involve the whole class and may include following up a strategy introduced before reading; completing a story map or doing the beach ball; acting out the story or "doing the book"; completing a graphic organizer or KWL chart; or drawing, writing, or discussing as a response to reading.

	SELF-SELECTED READING
Goals	■ To introduce students to all types of literature through the teacher read-aloud ■ To encourage students' reading interests ■ To provide instructional-level reading materials ■ To build students' intrinsic motivation for reading
Teacher Read-Aloud	■ The teacher chooses a book or selection to read aloud to all students. ■ The read-alouds include a variety of levels, genres, and authors.
Independent Reading and Conferencing	■ Students choose books or magazines at their levels and read them independently. ■ The teacher conferences with individual members of the class. ■ Conferences are student-directed; the student chooses one or two pages to read aloud and discuss with the teacher.
Sharing (Optional)	■ Students briefly share what they have read. ■ Sharing may take the form of reader's chair or share chair, table sharing, buddy sharing, four- square share, etc.

WRITING

Goals	<ul><li>To have students view writing as a way of telling about things</li><li>To develop fluent writing for all students</li><li>To teach students to use correct grammar and mechanics in their writing</li><li>To teach particular writing forms</li><li>To allow students to learn to read through writing</li><li>To maintain the motivation and self-confidence of struggling writers</li></ul>
Mini-Lesson	<ul><li>The teacher models writing.</li><li>Each mini-lesson has a focus that depends on the time of year and the needs of students.</li></ul>
Student Writing and Conferencing	<ul><li>Students write.</li><li>Some students are beginning new pieces; others are continuing work on pieces that take several days to write; still others are working on editing and publishing pieces.</li><li>The teacher conferences with individuals or small groups of students.</li></ul>
Sharing (Author's Chair)	<ul><li>Students share their writing with each other.</li><li>After students share, classmates make nice comments and ask questions.</li></ul>

WORKING WITH WORDS

Goals	<ul><li>To teach students how to read and spell high-frequency words</li><li>To teach students how to decode and spell other words using patterns from known words</li><li>To have students automatically and fluently use phonics and spelling patterns while reading and writing</li></ul>
Word Wall	<ul><li>The teacher chooses five words to focus on for the week, introducing them on the first day and focusing on new words or reviewing words already on the Word Wall as necessary throughout the week.</li><li>Each day, the teacher calls out five words and leads students in a rhythmic chant spelling of each word.</li><li>Next, students write the words.</li><li>After writing, the teacher leads students in checking their papers.</li><li>As students become faster at writing the words, the teacher may include an On-the-Back activity on the backs of their papers.</li></ul>
Phonics/ Spelling Patterns	<ul><li>Several different activities may be used here, including Making Words, Rounding Up the Rhymes, Reading/Writing Rhymes, Guess the Covered Word, and Using Words You Know.</li></ul>

What Does the Research Say?

The philosophy behind Four Blocks is based on solid research that has been proven in the past and is supported in the present.

What the Research Says about Teaching Reading	What Four Blocks Provides
"A combination of approaches is generally more effective in the teaching of reading than is the use of a single approach." (Bond & Dykstra, 1967)	Guided Reading, Self-Selected Reading, Writing, and Working with Words are used every day to reach every student.
"Students who are placed in the 'bottom' reading group in first grade generally remain there throughout elementary school and almost never learn to read and write on level." (Allington, 1983; 1991)	Success is provided for all students without using ability-level grouping.

What the Research Says about Guided Oral Reading	In the Guided Reading Block
"What do the results of the meta-analysis of guided oral reading procedures show? . . . These data provide strong support for the supposition that instruction in guided oral reading is effective in improving reading." (National Reading Panel [NRP], p. 3-3)	Using examples based on real students's literature, Four Blocks shows teachers how to use a variety of strategies, including previewing the text, using graphic organizers, writing, and generating questions.
"Generally, the [National Reading] Panel found that [guided oral reading] procedures tended to improve word recognition, fluency (speed and accuracy of oral reading), and comprehension with most groups." (NRP, 2000, p. 3–28)	Making guided oral reading a meaningful activity will improve reader fluency.
"Historically, most of the instructional attention accorded to oral fluency was developed through round-robin reading, a still widely used approach in which teachers have students take turns reading parts of a text aloud . . . These procedures have been criticized as boring, anxiety provoking, disruptive of fluency, and wasteful of instructional time, and their use has been found to have little or no relationship to gains in reading achievement." (NRP, 2000, p. 3–11)	Students engage regularly in shared reading, repeated reading, and paired reading/peer tutoring/partner reading—almost never in round-robin reading.

What the Research Says about Self-Selected Reading	In the Self-Selected Reading Block
"Most theories are agreed that the bulk of vocabulary growth during a child's lifetime occurs indirectly through language exposure rather than through direct teaching . . . Furthermore, many researchers are convinced that reading volume, rather than oral language, is the prime contributor to individual differences in students's vocabularies . . ." (A. Cunningham and Stanovich, 1998, p. 9)	Teachers guide students in developing strategies for determining which books are appropriate for Self-Selected Reading.
"Increasing the amount of reading students do is important, because as words are encountered repeatedly there are a number of beneficial outcomes, such as improvements in word recognition, speed, ease of reading, and comprehension." (Topping & Paul, 1999, and A. Cunningham & Stanovich, 1998)	Students have many opportunities to read and learn that reading is valuable enough for classroom time to be devoted to it.

What the Research Says about Writing	In the Writing Block
"Natural process writing is more effective [than grammar instruction and traditional, presentational writing instruction,] and what has been called environmental writing instruction, where students engage in various writing activities designed to teach them to learn and apply specific writing strategies, is more effective still." (Hillocks, 1986)	The framework emphasizes self-selected writing in second grade, and it makes writing much more environmental.
"Teaching students to write legibly increases their writing fluency." (Graham, Harris, & Fink, 2000)	Handwriting and spelling skills are taught systematically in the Working with Words Block and are used in the Writing Block.

What the Research Says about Phonemic Awareness	In the Working with Words Block
"PA training programs varied . . . in the type of phoneme manipulations taught, segmenting, blending, deleting, identifying, or categorizing phoneme, or manipulating onsets or rimes." (NRP, 2000, p. 2-28)	In second grade, students continue to segment spoken words into phonemes in the various Working with Words activities. They apply this skill during the Writing Block.
"Phonemic awareness is one of the best predictors of success in learning to read." (Bryant, Bradley, MacLean, and Crossland, 1989)	Students are taught to segment spoken words into phonemes in Working with Words activities and apply this skill during the Writing Block.

What the Research Says about Phonics	In the Working with Words Block
"The greatest improvements were seen from systematic phonics instruction. This type of phonics instruction consists of teaching a planned sequence of phonics elements, rather than highlighting elements as they happen to appear in a text." (Langenberg, 2000)	Systematic phonics instruction includes a planned sequence of phonics lessons in which students first learn phonemic awareness, letter names, and sounds. Then, they progress to digraphs, blends, and vowel patterns in one- and two-syllable words.
"Teachers may be expected to use a particular phonics program with their class, yet it quickly becomes apparent that the program suits some students more than others. In the early grades, students are known to vary greatly in the skills they bring to school. There will be some students who already know the letter-sound correspondences, some students who can decode words, and others who have little or no knowledge. Should teachers proceed through the program and ignore these students?" (NRP, 2000, p. 2–136)	Phonics is planned, sequential, and multi-level. Each lesson has a focus and provides something for late bloomers and early developers.

What the Research Says about Vocabulary Learning	In All Four Blocks
"Dependence on a single vocabulary instruction method will not result in optimal learning." (NRP, 2000, p. 4-4 and 4-27)	Students receive both direct/explicit instruction, such as word meanings before Guided Reading, and indirect/indirect instruction through Self-Selected reading, teacher read-alouds, and talking about books.
"When vocabulary items are derived from content learning materials, the learner will be better equipped to deal with specific reading matter in content areas." (NRP, 2000, p. 4-4)	Four Blocks uses reading in the content areas as much as possible and, unlike a reading and writing approach that uses leveled groups, leaves time for teaching in the content areas.

Reading Standards Chart

	GUIDED READING	SELF-SELECTED READING	WRITING	WORKING WITH WORDS
Phonemic Awareness				
Identify and isolate initial, medial, and final sounds of spoken words. **CA1.1, TX110.4.b.5(A,D)**				■
Blend initial letter-sounds with common vowel spelling patterns to read words. **TX110.4.b.5(B)**				■
Listening				
Connect experiences and ideas with those of others through speaking, listening, and questioning. **TX110.4.b.2(A), FL LA.C.3.1.2, FL LAC.3.1.3**	■	■	■	
Listen critically to interpret and evaluate. **TX110.4.b.1(D)**	■	■	■	
Ask and answer relevant questions and make contributions in small- or large-group discussions. **TX110.4.b.3(C)**	■	■	■	■
Decoding and Word Recognition				
Recognize high-frequency irregular words. **CA1.3, TX110.4.b.5(C)**	■	■		■
Use knowledge of prefixes, suffixes, and inflectional endings to determine the meanings of words. **FL LA.A.1.1.3, TX110.4.b.3(E,F), CA1.5, CA1.9**	■	■		■

	GUIDED READING	SELF-SELECTED READING	WRITING	WORKING WITH WORDS
Comprehension				
Respond to who, what, when, where, and how questions. **CA2.4**	■		■	
Recognize cause-and-effect relationships in text. **CA2.6**	■	■		
Relate prior knowledge to textual information. **TX110.4.b.9(A)**	■	■	■	
Use strategies to increase comprehension. **FL LA.A.1.1.4, TX110.4.b.9(C,D,E,F,H)**	■	■		
Self-select reading materials by drawing on personal interest, by relying on knowledge of authors and different types of texts, and/or by estimating text difficulty. **TX110.4.b.6(A,D), FL LA.A.2.1.2**		■		
Increase comprehension by rereading, retelling, and discussing. **FL LA.A.1.1.4, TX110.4.b.9(C), CA2.5**	■	■		
Vocabulary and Concept Development				
Discuss meanings of words and develop vocabulary through meaningful/concrete experiences. **TX110.4.b.8(A)**	■	■		■
Develop vocabulary by listening to and discussing both familiar and conceptually challenging selections. **TX110.4.b.8(B), FL LA.A.1.1.3(5)**	■	■		■
Writing				
Use writing strategies (brainstorming, discussion, graphic organizers, etc.) to develop a central idea. **CA1.1, TX110.4.b.18(A,B), FL LA.B.1.1.1**	■		■	
Write legibly and space letters, words, and sentences appropriately. **CA1.2, FL LA.B.1.1.2(2), TX110.4.b.15(A,B)**	■		■	■
Use descriptive language when writing. **CA 1.4, FL LA.B.1.1.2**			■	

Summary of the Guided Reading Block

The purposes of this block are to build students' comprehension and fluency with reading and to introduce students to a variety of literature, including stories, informational text, and poetry.

For more information on these activities and how to complete them with your class, see The Guided Reading Block, pages 44–77.

Total Time: 30—40 minutes

Before Reading

10 min.

1. Introduce and support grade-level and easier text in a number of ways over multiple days:
   - build on students' prior knowledge about the text and topic
   - begin graphic organizers, such as webs and story maps
   - guide picture discussion and prediction
   - discuss key vocabulary

2. Focus the lesson on a comprehension skill or strategy.

During Reading

15-20 min.

1. Provide a variety of formats for reading the text. Grouping may be paired (partner), individual, small groups, whole group, Three-Ring Circus, or Book Club groups and can include special teachers or volunteers.

2. Students read the selections. Listen to their reading, coach those who need help, and occasionally take anecdotal notes.

After Reading

5-10 min.

Direct the whole group in closure activities to match the purpose. These activities may include the following:
   - discussing what was read
   - acting out the story
   - drawing or writing in response to reading
   - completing a KWL chart or graphic organizer

A Typical Week in the Guided Reading Block

MONDAY

Grade-Level Selection: *Penguins!* by Gail Gibbons

Before Reading

- **Activate Prior Knowledge:** Talk about a visit to an aquarium or a zoo where you saw a penguin exhibit. Ask students if they have ever seen penguins at an aquarium or a zoo or on TV.

- **KWL Chart:** On a large piece of chart paper, label three columns **K**, **W**, and **L**. Ask students to share what they already Know about penguins. As students talk, write their responses under the **K** column. Next, ask students what they Want to learn about penguins and record what they say under the **W** column.

- **Teacher-Supported Reading:** Invite students to join in an echo reading of the first two pages of text. Point out the labeled illustrations and have students echo read these too. Note facts that you might like to add to the KWL chart when you are finished reading.

- **Set a Purpose:** Explain to students that as they read today, they will look for answers to any questions listed under the **W** column of their KWL chart and to see what they can add to the **L** column.

During Reading

- Ask students to read half of the text with their assigned partners. Pass out sticky notes and remind students to look for interesting penguin facts to add to the KWL chart as they read. Have students read the story in assigned pairs—stronger readers with struggling ones when possible. Move around the room, listening to partners and coaching as needed. As pairs finish reading, they talk about the things they have learned, write on their sticky notes, and put the sticky notes on the pages where they found the information.

After Reading

- Call students to the front of the room. Students use the sticky notes to add the things they have Learned to the **L** column of the KWL chart.

Grade-Level Selection: *Penguins!* by Gail Gibbons

Before Reading

■ **Activate Prior Knowledge:** Review the KWL chart. Students will add new information from their reading to this chart today.

■ **Set a Purpose:** Tell students that they will add other interesting things they learn about penguins to the KWL chart today when they finish reading the book with partners.

During Reading

■ Students finish reading the book with their partners from yesterday. Everyone has sticky notes during reading to mark important information that should be added to the KWL chart. Give students 15 minutes to finish reading and to write on their sticky notes.

After Reading

■ Let each set of partners use their sticky notes to share what they have learned. Add the new information to the KWL chart. Explain that during center time today or tomorrow, pairs of students will go to the writing center. If there is time, each student should choose one fact from the KWL chart to write and illustrate. The students' pages will be put together to make a class book.

Grade-Level Selection: *Penguins!* by Gail Gibbons

Before Reading

- **Activate Prior Knowledge:** Explain that some books are about things that have not really happened; they are made-up stories that are called fiction. Other selections are written about real people, animals, things, and events that are called nonfiction. List two headings, Fiction and Nonfiction, on the board and give an example of each. List some features under the headings. Ask students whether *Penguins* is fiction or nonfiction and why. Discuss this. Students decide that this book is a nonfiction selection because it gives the reader facts about real penguins.

- Draw a web on the board and put the word **penguins** in the middle as the topic word. Draw spokes from the center circle to seven smaller circles with the words **appearance**, **home**, **food**, **moving**, **babies**, and **dangers** and the phrase **staying warm**. Add spokes to these smaller circles. Tell students, "After rereading today, we will add to these spokes."

- **Set a Purpose:** Tell students, "While you read today, think about the things you learn about penguins in this nonfiction book. Think about where you would add these things to the web we have started. If you have time after reading, look back through the book and think about what you could add to each of the seven circles."

During Reading

- Use the Three-Ring Circus format to reread the selection. The most capable readers may read the story by themselves. You read the selection with a small group of students who need more guidance and coaching to read the book. But, in Four-Blocks fashion, make sure to add a capable reader to the group as a model. The remaining students are assigned new partners and will reread the book again with their new partners.

After Reading

- Call students together to sit in the front of the room. Take a minute to compliment and reinforce good reading behaviors that you saw during reading time. Then, let students share information about penguins to add to the seven circles. Add the information to the penguin web. If students did not have time to start or finish their pages for the class penguin book yesterday, let them do so now.

Easier Selection: *Tacky the Penguin* **by Helen Lester**

Before Reading

- **Activate Prior Knowledge:** Talk with students about the differences between fiction and nonfiction. Remind them that fiction books generally tell stories and nonfiction books give facts. Then, explain that you can also learn things about a topic from a fiction story. Tell students that today, they will read a fiction story about a penguin who is different from other penguins. This story is meant to entertain the reader, but it also gives the reader information about penguins.

- **Picture Walk:** Take students on a picture walk through the story, pointing out key vocabulary words, such as **companions**, **hearty**, **cannonballs**, **switch**, **gracefully**, and **dreadfully**. Call students' attention to the location of print on pages 8–9 and pages 24–25 and the all-capitalized and italicized words throughout the story. Ask students for suggestions about how these words should be read.

- **Comprehension Mini-Lesson:** Tell students that you will share with them something that good readers do when they read: they ask questions about their reading. Explain that this is something they do no matter how old they are or how difficult the book that they are reading is. Tell students that sometimes you ask questions because you don't understand something or you ask questions because you want to know more. Say, "During our picture walk, I thought of questions for *Tacky the Penguin*."

- **Set a Purpose:** Tell students that they will do an Everyone Read To . . . (ERT) for *Tacky the Penguin*. Through this method, students will read to **find** where the answer to the question is stated on the page. They will read to **figure out** when they must make inferences or to **figure out** the answer to a question.

During Reading

- Students whisper-read each two-page spread with partners, then discuss as a class the answer to each question. Have a volunteer read aloud the part of the page where the answer was found.
- **p. 3:**   Everyone Read To find where the penguin lives.
- **p. 4–5:**   Everyone Read To find who the characters are in the story. Which one is the "odd bird"?
- **p. 6–7:**   Everyone Read To figure out what the other penguins think of Tacky's greeting.
- **p. 7–10:**   Everyone Read To find if how Tacky marches and dives is the same as or different from how other penguins march and dive.
- **p. 12–13:** Everyone Read To figure out what the other penguins think of Tacky's song.
- **p. 14–15:** Everyone Read To find who makes the thumping noise.
- **p. 16–17:** Everyone Read To find what the hunters bring.
- **p. 18–19:** Everyone Read To find what the other penguins do when they hear the hunters coming.
- **p. 20–21:** Everyone Read To find what the hunters want to do with the penguins.
- **p. 22–23:** Everyone Read To find what Tacky does while the others hide.
- **p. 24–25:** Everyone Read To figure out why the hunters are puzzled.
- **p. 26–27:** Everyone Read To figure out how the hunters get wet.
- **p. 28–29:** Everyone Read To figure out why the hunters are covering their ears.
- **p. 30–31:** Everyone Read To find why the hunters run away.
- **p. 32:**   Everyone Read To figure out how the penguins feel about Tacky.

THURSDAY

After Reading

■ Conclude the lesson by discussing what happens in the story. Toss the beach ball and have students answer the questions on it. Who are the characters? What is the setting? What happens in the story? Tell the class that tomorrow you will reread this book and act out the story.

FRIDAY

Easier Selection: *Tacky the Penguin* **by Helen Lester**

Before Reading

■ **Activate Prior Knowledge:** Remind students that today, they will "do the book." Prior to the lesson, copy a picture of each penguin and hunter character in the book and glue it to cardboard. Write the name of the character, punch two holes at the top, and thread yarn through each card so that students can wear the character cards around their necks. To begin, place the cards on the board's ledge. Lead students in a discussion of each character. Students flip through the story to see what each character says, how the dialogue should be said, and what actions the characters perform.

■ **Set a Purpose:** Tell students that some students will "do the book" and have a part in this play and that others will watch. If there is enough time, students who watched the first time will be given parts, and the performers will become the audience as you "do the book" one more time.

During Reading

■ Distribute the character cards for the penguins and the hunters in this story and have students come to the front of the classroom. Students become the characters and act out the story. The story is read twice if time permits so that all students may have opportunities for roles in the play.

After Reading

■ As the whole class reconvenes, take a minute to compliment both the acting and narration of the story. Let students discuss their favorite parts of the play(s). Toward the end of the week, tell students that both Gail Gibbons and Helen Lester have written many other books, including more *Tacky* books, and that one or both of these authors might be a Book Club possibility in the future.

Teacher's Self-Evaluation for Guided Reading

Here are some questions to ask yourself to determine how well you are leading Guided Reading and to help you grow in this block.

_____ **1.** Am I including different kinds of literature—stories, informational books, mysteries, biographies, old favorites, chapter books, poetry, plays, etc.?

_____ **2.** Am I including grade-level and easier materials?

_____ **3.** Am I using a variety of materials to prepare students before they read?

_____ **4.** Am I helping students access and build prior knowledge and important meaning vocabulary?

_____ **5.** Am I setting a clear purpose for reading so that students know exactly what they will do after reading and read to get ready to do that?

_____ **6.** Am I using a variety of during-reading formats to provide the support necessary for all of my students to succeed in reading the text for the purpose I set?

_____ **7.** Am I modeling and role-playing the formats (partner reading, Book Club Groups, etc.) so that students know exactly what is expected of them?

_____ **8.** Am I using my time while students read to monitor, assess, and coach students in ways appropriate to the format I am using?

_____ **9.** Do I set and stick to reasonable time limits for students' reading and make it clear to them what to do if they finish reading before the time is up?

_____ **10.** Do I immediately follow up the purpose I set for reading so that students "take me seriously" when I tell them what they will need to be ready to do after we read?

_____ **11.** Does my after-reading activity focus on comprehension and help students learn how to think as they read?

_____ **12.** Do I seek out or create Guided Reading materials that connect to my science and social studies topics?

_____ **13.** Am I pacing this block so that it is completed in 30–40 minutes each day?

Making the Guided Reading Block Multilevel

Guided Reading is the hardest block to make multilevel. Any reading selection will be too hard for some students and too easy for others. There is no need to worry about those students for whom grade-level Guided Reading material is too easy, because the other three blocks take up three-quarters of their block time and provide many beyond-grade-level opportunities. In addition, end-of-year testing always indicates that students in Four-Blocks classes who begin second grade with high literacy levels read well above grade level at the end of the year.

When using Book Club Groups, you do, however, need to be concerned about those students for whom grade-level selections are too hard. To make this block meet the needs of students who read below grade level, you can make a variety of adaptations. **Guided Reading time is not spent on grade-level material all week**. Rather, you choose two selections—one at the average reading level of the class and one that is easier—to read each week. The shared reading of a big book is always a good selection for the easier reading. When using Book Club Groups, you should try to have one choice be an easier—but still appealing—book. When reading longer selections in second grade, it may take several days to complete them; so, it is possible to spend a week, more or less, on a grade-level selection or a week on an easier selection.

When using a picture book or short story, the class can read the selection more than once, reading each time for a different purpose in a different format. Rereading enables students who could not read it fluently the first time to achieve fluency by the last reading. This rereading is not always possible with longer selections in second grade. Students who need help are not left to read by themselves but are supported in a variety of ways. Most teachers use reading partners and teach students how to help their partners, rather than do all of their reading for them. The Three-Ring Circus format has some students read the selection by themselves and others read with partners, while the teacher meets with a small group of students to help them with the reading and comprehension. This variety of formats helps below-level readers achieve some success and learn important reading strategies.

Teachers also provide additional easy-reading time for students whose reading level is well below even the easier selections. You may meet with students individually or in small groups while the rest of your students are engaged in other activities. Or, you may arrange for tutors to work individually with students or coordinate with early-intervention teachers. One way or another, you should make sure that students are getting the support they need, including some coaching each week as they read material at their instructional levels.

Summary of the Self-Selected Reading Block

The purposes of this block are to build students' fluency in reading, to allow students to read and enjoy text that is appropriate to their independent reading levels, and to build confidence in students as readers.

For more information on these activities and how to complete them with your class, see The Self-Selected Reading Block, pages 78-91.

Total Time: 30–40 minutes

Teacher Read-Aloud

Read aloud to all students from a variety of genres, topics, and authors.

10 min.

Independent Reading and Conferencing

1. Students either move to a reading area and select books or choose books or magazines from the baskets at their tables to read independently.

2. Hold conferences with three to five students daily as the other students read. Keep a conference form for recording each student's progress, preferences, and responses.

15-20 min.

Sharing

1. Several students share briefly (approximately two minutes each) with the whole class what they have read.

2. If time allows, the reader answers several questions from classmates about the book. Model the types of thoughtful questions that students should ask.

5-10 min.

A Typical Week in the Self-Selected Reading Block

MONDAY

> **Read-aloud title:** *The Little Penguin* by A. J. Wood (or any other fiction book about penguins)

Teacher Read-Aloud

- Gather students around your rocking chair, or another comfortable chair, in a carpeted area of the classroom. Since the class has begun a unit on penguins, tell students that you want to share a new book about penguins. Students listen attentively to the book and are drawn in by the lovable characters.

- Remind students that you have gathered a collection of printed materials—books, magazines, pamphlets, etc.—that relate to the week's theme of penguins. One group has the option of spending their Self-Selected Reading time in the center exploring those materials or remaining at their desks reading materials from the book baskets. Dismiss each table of students one at a time to go quietly to their places to read. Students who conferenced with you on Friday are allowed to go to the reading center.

Independent Reading and Conferencing

- Students make independent selections of books and settle down to read. Several students are involved in reading chapter books. Their books are in the baskets at their tables with personalized bookmarks holding the correct places.

- Have conferences (three to four minutes each) with one-fifth of your students about their books. Keep a record of the progress of each student. After 15 to 20 minutes of reading/conference time, alert students that the reading time has ended.

Sharing

- Students gather in a carpeted area where a cardboard TV front hangs from the ceiling at a height appropriate to frame a child sitting on a stool. Ask two students to "appear on TV" to share about the books they are reading and tell why they would recommend the books to others.

Read-aloud title: *Flip and Flop* **by Dawn Apperley (or any other fiction book about penguins)**

Teacher Read-Aloud

■ Gather students around your chair for the read-aloud. Once students are settled and quiet, tell them that you will read a book that is similar to the one the class is reading in the Guided Reading Block. It is about two penguins who are brothers. What adventures will they get into in their chilly home? Students listen quietly as you read the story and show the colorful illustrations.

■ As you dismiss students to begin their independent reading time, invite the Monday conference group to go to the reading center to explore the theme-related books located there. The other students return to their tables to choose books from the book baskets.

Independent Reading and Conferencing

■ Students read quietly while you conference with each student on the Tuesday list. Set a timer to help you pace.

Sharing

■ Two students sit in the Share Chair today and talk about their books, bringing closure to the Self-Selected Reading Block for the day.

Read-aloud title: *March of the Penguins* **by Luc Jacquet and Jerome Maison (or any other nonfiction book about penguins)**

Teacher Read-Aloud

■ Gather students around the chair. Remind them of the theme they have been studying (penguins) and of the selection they have been reading during the Guided Reading Block. "Many books we have been reading contain a lot of interesting facts about penguins. Today's book is a true story about the long journey some penguins make every year to their nesting grounds. You may have seen the movie that is based on this book. Let's see how the book compares to the movie!"

Independent Reading and Conferencing

■ Students with whom you conferenced Tuesday go to the reading center, and the other students return to their tables to read.

■ Hold conferences with students on your Wednesday list.

Sharing

■ Two students share their books in the Share Chair.

Read-aloud title: *Antarctica* **by David Petersen (or any other nonfiction book about penguins or Antarctica)**

Teacher Read-Aloud

■ Students may want to learn more about Antarctica after their science segment today, and this selection tells about the southernmost continent. Point out the many facts about Antarctica and encourage students to add to a web you made earlier. "What new things can we learn about Antarctica?" Students will be drawn in by the beautiful photographs in this book, as well as by the many interesting facts.

Independent Reading and Conferencing

■ Wednesday's conference students go to the reading center to explore books about travel and related topics, and the other students return to their tables to choose books from the book baskets.

■ Hold conferences with students on the Thursday list.

Sharing

■ Two students share their books in the Share Chair.

Read-aloud title: *Tacky in Trouble* by Helen Lester (or any other book in the *Tacky* series)

Teacher Read-Aloud

- Tell students that you have a story to read that will make them laugh. This is a sequel to the book *Tacky the Penguin*. "What type of trouble do you think Tacky is in this time?" Students enjoy the funny story.

Independent Reading and Conferencing

- Students who conferenced with you on Thursday go to the reading center.
- Conference with students on your Friday list as the other students read books from the baskets silently.

Sharing

- Partner students to share their books with book talk buddies. Students take their books with them so that they can show what the books look like, share how they're illustrated, and tell what they liked about them.

Teacher's Self-Evaluation for Self-Selected Reading

Here are some questions to ask yourself to determine how well you are doing Self-Selected Reading and to help you grow in this block.

_____ 1. Am I reading different kinds of literature—stories, informational books, mysteries, biographies, old favorites, chapter books, poetry, etc.?

_____ 2. Am I including some "quick reads" from magazines, newspapers, encyclopedias, Web sites, and other sources to show students that people read more than just books?

_____ 3. Am I reading materials at different levels—some at grade level, some above grade level, and some easy books—to model that all levels of books are acceptable?

_____ 4. Am I reading expressively and in an excited manner—stopping and commenting on things I particularly like or find fascinating and modeling daily the pleasure I get from reading?

_____ 5. Have I gathered the widest amount and variety of materials for my students to select from, using school and public library sources if necessary to have what I need?

_____ 6. Do I have interesting, easy, and challenging books so that all of my students can find something on their level that they want to read?

_____ 7. Are the books easily accessible to students so that they don't have to wander from place to place to get books and waste reading time?

_____ 8. Do students move quickly into their reading, and do they stay engaged?

_____ 9. Early in the year, do I circulate and encourage students in their reading?

_____ 10. As the year progresses, do I conference with a portion of my students daily (often one-fifth of the class each day—fewer students if an unusually large class; more often if an unusually small class)?

_____ 11. Have I spread out struggling readers across the conference days, and am I giving them a little extra time to "ooh" and "aah" about their reading, as well as helping them choose books that they can read and will enjoy?

_____ 12. Have I spread out my advanced readers across the conference days, and do I occasionally suggest to them more challenging books that I think they can handle and will enjoy?

_____ 13. Do I have conversations (rather than interrogations) with my students, and do they look forward to their one-to-one book-talk time with me?

_____ 14. Do I make a record of the books students chose to conference on and indicate how well they read and understood the books?

_____ 15. Do I provide time for occasional sharing and set up the sharing so that students and I enjoy it and so that it motivates students to expand their reading interests?

_____ 16. Have I chosen some read-aloud materials, as well as some materials available for students to read that connect to my science and social studies topics?

_____ 17. Have I paced this block so that it is completed in 30-40 minutes?

Making the Self-Selected Reading Block Multilevel

Self-Selected Reading is, by definition, multilevel. **The component of Self-Selected Reading that makes it multilevel is that students choose what they want to read.** These choices, however, can be limited by what reading materials are available and how willing and able students are to read from the available resources. **To make the Self-Selected Reading Block as multilevel as possible, collect the widest range of levels, topics, and genres of books available.** There should be both chapter books and very easy books in second grade. Read aloud a variety of books as well.

In weekly conferences with students, praise the reading of all students, steer struggling readers toward easy—but interesting—books, and direct advanced readers toward challenging books. Remember that the topic of a book is critical and that students will often read books that are too easy—or even too hard—for them if they are really interested in that topic or author. **Students should be encouraged to read on their levels, but remember that this is called Self-Selected Reading—the main goal is to have students selecting the books that will turn them into readers.**

Summary of the Writing Block

The purposes of this block are to help students see writing as a way to tell about things, to build students' fluency in writing, to help students learn to read through writing, to have students apply grammar and mechanics in writing, to teach particular forms of writing, and to maintain the motivation and self-confidence of struggling writers.

For more information on these activities and how to complete them with your class, see The Writing Block, pages 92-117.

Total Time: 30—40 minutes

5-10 min.

Mini-Lesson—Teacher Writing

Present a mini-lesson in which you model real writing and a skill or strategy.

- Focus on writing, adding to, or editing a piece.

- Reference the Word Wall and other places in the room to model how words available in the room can help with spelling.

- Model the use of an Editor's Checklist to promote and guide self-checking, peer revision, and editing. This checklist grows as appropriate expectations are added throughout the year.

20 min.

Student Writing and Conferencing

1. Students write on self-selected topics, individually paced at various stages of the writing process, perhaps working for multiple days on one piece.

2. Hold individual conferences with some students while other students write. Each student picks one piece from three to five good first drafts to revise, edit, and publish after conferencing with the teacher.

5-10 min.

Sharing (Author's Chair)

1. Selected students use the Author's Chair to briefly share something they have written.

2. The author answers several questions from classmates about the writing. Model the types of thoughtful questions students should learn to ask each other.

A Typical Week in the Writing Block

MONDAY

Mini-Lesson on Combining Sentences

1. Call students to sit around the overhead. Brainstorm aloud about what you might write: "I could tell you about what I did this weekend, or I could tell you about the new puppy my friend just got. When we started our unit on penguins this morning, I began to think about how cold it is where penguins live. I think that winter is what I really want to write about today!"

2. Begin to write on a lined transparency. Occasionally, come to a word that you have to "stretch out" by the way it sounds. Continue to compose a story about winter, making sure to include some short, choppy sentences.

3. When you have finished your draft, read it aloud to students. Then, say, "When I was reading my piece aloud, I noticed that I had used some short, choppy sentences. I will combine some of these sentences to make them a little more interesting. Watch as I try that with these two sentences."

4. Make the changes and reread the piece. Tell students that you like it much better.

5. Dismiss students to do their own writing: "Those of you who are starting new pieces can go back to your seats and get started. Those of you who are adding on to pieces can go back and continue writing. Those of you who are ready to revise and edit can go back to your seats and begin. Those of you who are publishing can go to the publishing table. I need Maddie to come with me to finish the editing we started yesterday. Bern will be next after Maddie finishes."

Writing

- Students work on different stages of their writing while you have brief conferences with students who are ready to publish. When the timer sounds, students put away their work and come to the sharing area to hear what their classmates have written.

Author's Chair

- The students on your Monday list take turns in the Author's Chair. After each student reads, a few class-mates comment on what they like and ask questions. Occasionally, you model thoughtful questions that will help students think about their writing.

Mini-Lesson on Adding On to a Piece

1. Call students to sit around the overhead and say, "Yesterday, I wrote about winter, but I didn't get to write everything that I wanted. I need to find a way to continue writing so that I can add some other things I want to say."

2. Next, take out the transparency from the Monday lesson. Read it aloud. Say, "The first thing I should do before I start writing more is read what I have already written. Then, I should try to think of other things I can write. I could write about my favorite winter holiday or the different clothes I wear during winter."

3. Write a new paragraph that tells about winter. After you finish, read what you have written aloud. Tell students that you are glad that you were able to write more and give more information about winter.

4. Have students help you edit your piece using the Editor's Checklist.

Writing

■ Students work at different stages of their writing while you have brief conferences.

Author's Chair

■ The Tuesday students share their writing in the Author's Chair.

Mini-Lesson on Choosing a Topic

1. Call students to sit around the overhead. Think aloud about what you will write today.

2. After several ideas, you decide that you will write about your trip to the zoo to see the penguins. Begin to write about the many types of penguins you saw at the zoo and how interesting it was to learn about them.

3. After you finish your piece, reread it and say, "The same thing happened in my story that sometimes happens in your stories. I have written a sentence that goes on and on. This is called a run-on sentence. I think that I'll fix it."

4. Change the run-on sentence into two good sentences.

Writing

■ Students work at different stages of their writing while you have brief conferences.

Author's Chair

■ The Wednesday students share their writing in the Author's Chair.

Mini-Lesson on Writing a Summary

1. Call students to sit around the overhead. Bring the web that the class made yesterday in Guided Reading after talking about penguins. The web is a class-generated list of facts about penguins. Students have also read a book in Self-Selected Reading called *March of the Penguins* by Luc Jacquet.

2. Explain that you will use the web to write a summary about penguins. Show students how to organize the ideas into a summary. Write a lead paragraph and another good paragraph and say, "I'll need to continue this tomorrow and write about some other important facts."

Writing

■ Students work at different stages of their writing while you have brief conferences.

Author's Chair

■ The Thursday students share their writing in the Author's Chair.

FRIDAY

Mini-Lesson on Writing a Summary, *continued*

■ Call students to sit around the overhead. Remind them that you need to continue the summary that you started on Thursday. Reread your sentences and add another paragraph and a good ending. Finally, ask the class to help you edit the piece using the Editor's Checklist.

Writing

■ Students work at different stages of their writing while you have brief conferences.

Author's Chair

■ The Friday students share their writing in the Author's Chair.

Teacher's Self-Evaluation for Writing

Here are some questions to ask yourself to determine how well you are doing Writing and to help you grow in this block.

_____ **1.** Do I gather students together each day for my mini-lesson, modeling how to write as I write and talking about how I think as I write?

_____ **2.** Am I focusing my mini-lesson on the one thing that I have chosen to help my students move forward in their writing?

_____ **3.** Am I doing several mini-lessons with the same focus so that students will learn how to do what I am focusing on?

_____ **4.** Am I looking at my students' writing and at our curriculum to decide on appropriate mini-lessons?

_____ **5.** Am I letting students choose their topics for writing and encouraging them to take as many days as needed to write each piece?

_____ **6.** Am I using my time while students are writing to conference with students, encouraging them in their efforts early in the year and helping them revise, edit, and publish as the year goes on?

_____ **7.** Am I helping students select which pieces to publish, rather than publishing everything (even if they want to)?

_____ **8.** Am I providing opportunities for students to share what they write with each other and modeling positive comments and thoughtful questions in response to their writing?

_____ **9.** As the year goes on, am I including some focused writing lessons in which students learn to write in particular forms?

_____ **10.** Am I teaching students how to edit their writing and, as the year goes on, how to peer edit?

_____ **11.** Am I including appropriate grammar and mechanics in my mini-lessons and on my Editor's Checklist, as well as teaching students to apply these in their writing?

_____ **12.** On some days during my mini-lesson, am I writing about science and social studies topics and encouraging my students to do so, as well, if they choose?

_____ **13.** Have I paced this block so that it is completed in 30-40 minutes?

Making the Writing Block Multilevel

Writing is already a multilevel block because it is not limited by the availability or acceptability of appropriate books. If you allow students to choose their own topics, accept whatever level of first-draft writing each student can accomplish, and allow students to work on their pieces as many days as needed; all students can succeed in writing.

One of the major tenets of process writing is that students should choose their own topics. When students decide what they will write, they write about something of particular interest to them and consequently something that they know about. This may seem like belaboring the obvious, but it is a crucial component in making the writing process multilevel. When everyone writes about the same topic, the different levels of students' knowledge and writing ability become painfully obvious. **If students write about topics that interest them, they are more likely to succeed, as in this example:**

In one classroom, two boys each took a turn in the Author's Chair on the same day. Jake, a very advanced writer, read a book he had authored, titled *Rocks*. His 16-page book contained illustrations and detailed descriptions of metamorphic, igneous, and sedimentary rocks. The next author was Cody, one of the struggling readers and writers in the classroom. He proudly read his eight-page illustrated book, titled *My New Bike*. When the two boys read, the difference in their literacy levels was striking.

Later, several of the other students in the class were individually asked what they liked about the two pieces, and how they were different. Students replied, "Jake wrote about rocks, and Cody wrote about his bike." Opinions about the pieces were divided, but most students seemed to prefer the bike piece to the rock piece—bikes being of greater interest than rocks to most students!

Writing is multilevel when students choose their topics and write about what they know. The differences in the writing levels of students are obvious to adults, but students tend to focus on the topic and not notice the different writing levels.

Writing is also multilevel because, for some students, writing is the best avenue to becoming readers. When students who are struggling with reading write about their own experiences and read it back (even if no one else can read it!), they are using their own language and experiences to become readers. Often, these students, who struggle with even the simplest material during Guided Reading, can read everything in their writing notebooks or folders. When students are writing, some of them are really working on becoming better writers; others are engaging in the same activity, but for them, writing is how they figure out reading.

In addition to teacher acceptance, students' choosing their own topics, and teachers' not expecting finished pieces each day, the Writing Block includes two teaching opportunities that promote the multilevel function of process writing: mini-lessons and conferences.

In mini-lessons, you write and students get to watch you thinking as you write. In these daily short lessons, you show all aspects of the writing process. You model topic selection, planning, writing, revising, and editing. You also write on a variety of topics in different forms. Some days, you write short pieces. Other days, you work on pieces that take several days to complete. When doing longer pieces, you model how to reread previous writing in order to pick up the train of thought and continue writing.

Mini-lessons contribute to making writing multilevel when the following occur:

- **All facets of the writing process are included.**

- **The teacher writes on a variety of topics in a variety of forms.**

- **The teacher intentionally writes some shorter, easier pieces and some more involved, longer pieces.**

Another opportunity for meeting the various needs and levels of students comes in the writing conference. In some classrooms, as students develop in their writing, they do some peer revising and editing and come to the teacher ("editor-in-chief") for final revisions before publishing. By helping students publish their work, you have the opportunity to truly individualize your teaching. Looking at the student's writing usually reveals both what the student needs to move forward and what the student is ready to understand. The writing conference provides the "teachable moment" in which both advanced and struggling writers can be nudged forward in their literacy development.

Another way to ensure that the Writing Block is a successful experience for all levels of writers is to spend a minute or two with a struggling reader before that student shares her work in the Author's Chair. If the student wants to share from a first-draft piece but is unable to read it and you can't read it either, you can coach the student to "tell" her piece rather than trying to read it. If a struggling reader is about to read from a published piece for which you have provided a lot of help, you can practice-read it with the student a time or two to ensure that he can read it fluently when in the Author's Chair.

Summary of the Working with Words Block

The purposes of this block are to ensure that students read, spell, and use high-frequency words correctly and that they learn the patterns necessary for decoding and spelling.

For more information on these activities and how to complete them with your class, see The Working with Words Block, pages 118-155.

Total Time: 30 minutes (Pacing is critical!)

Word Wall

Introduce five Word Wall words each week by having students do the following:
- See the words.
- Say the words.
- Chant the words (snap, clap, stomp, cheer, etc.).
- Write the words and check them with you.
- Do On-the-Back activities involving the words.

On days of the week when new Word Wall words are not the focus, review previous Word Wall words. When students can cheer for, write, and check five words in less than 10 minutes, the remaining minutes are used for an On-the-Back activity.

Decoding/Spelling Activity

Guide activities to help students learn spelling patterns. Activities may include any of the following:
- **Making Words,** in which students manipulate letters to construct words, sort words into patterns, and use the sorted rhyming words to spell and read new words
- **Guess the Covered Word,** which helps students learn to cross-check meaning and letter-sound relationships to figure out the covered words in sentences
- **Using Words You Know,** in which students learn how the words they already know can help them read and spell other words
- **Rounding Up the Rhymes,** which emphasizes spelling and rhyming patterns
- **Reading/Writing Rhymes,** in which students use rhyming words to write and read some silly rhymes
- Other activities that help students learn and use patterns to decode and spell words (Cunningham, 2008)

A Typical Week in the Working with Words Block

MONDAY

Word Wall

■ Introduce five new words. As each word is shown, students say the word, chant it, write it, trace around the word, and check it with you. When they complete that, lead students in a quick On-the-Back activity in which they write the five words in alphabetical order.

Making Words

■ Lead students in a Making Words activity using the theme-connected word **penguins** as the secret word. The activity leads them through making 14 words:

Make:	in	pin	pigs	spine	genius	penguins
		pen	pens	unpin		
		peg	pins	using		
		pig	pine			

Sort: The class then sorts for plurals (adding s) and for __**in** and __**ine**.

Transfer: The class uses rhyming words to figure out how to read and spell the transfer words **shin**, **twin**, **vine**, and **whine**.

Word Wall

■ Review five Word Wall words. Students say, clap, chant, write, and trace around these five words. Then, lead students in an On-the-Back activity in which they practice how one of the words, **right**, can help them spell five other words: **fight**, **light**, **might**, **bright**, and **fright**.

Using Words You Know

■ Lead the class in a Using Words You Know activity in which they use **name**, **day**, **back**, and **thump** to read and spell the following words.

■ **Words to Read:** game, play, stack, dump, lump, Zack, stay, fame, frame, Ray, stump, tray, clump, same, pray, rack, backpack

■ **Words to Write:** pay, pump, black, tame, blame, track, hump, clay, flame, sway, crack, bump, payday

---

WEDNESDAY

Word Wall

■ Review five Word Wall words and then lead students in a Be a Mind Reader activity on the backs of their papers.

Reading/Writing Rhymes with __ap

■ Create a Reading/Writing Rhymes chart with the class using ___**ap.** Ask students to suggest onsets until all of the slots on your chart are filled. Your finished chart might look like this:

Hap	flap	tap	rap	wrap	scrap
cap	trap	nap	lap	slap	map

■ Once you have completed the chart, work together with the class in a shared writing format to come up with a silly sentence that uses several of the rhyming words like the following.

Hap wears a cap with a flap as he sings a rap with a slap to his lap.

■ Next, have students work in pairs to come up with more silly sentences using the rhyming words on the chart. When they are finished, partners may share their rhymes with the class.

Word Wall

- Review five Word Wall words, especially any words with which students are having difficulty in their writing. Then, lead students to see how the words **write** and **want** are spelled when endings are added. Have students write **writer**, **writing**, **wants**, **wanted**, and **wanting** in their On-the-Back activity.

Making Words

- Lead students in a Making Words activity using the theme-connected word **feathers** as the secret word. The activity leads them through making 16 words.

Make:	at	her	seat	heart	father	fathers	feathers
	he	hat	feat	sheet			
	rat	feet	these				
	sat	heat					

Sort: The class sorts for plurals (adding s) and for homophones (feat, feet) with the ___at, ___eat, and ___eet rhyming patterns.

Transfer: Students use the rhyming words to figure out how to read and spell the transfer words **scat**, **wheat**, **tweet**, and **cats**.

Word Wall

- Five starred words are called out, cheered for, and written. On the backs of their papers, students decide which of the words they wrote on the front—**phone**, **drink**, **car**, **quit**, **trip**—will help them spell **bone**, **think**, **scar**, **skit**, and **chip**.

Guess the Covered Word

- Lead the class in a Guess the Covered Word activity. The sentences reinforce facts the class has learned about penguins throughout the week.

  1. Some penguins live in **zoos**.
  2. Penguins **waddle** on the land.
  3. They swim in the **sea**.
  4. Some penguins build nests with **stones**.
  5. A chick is cared for by its **parents**.

Teacher's Self-Evaluation for Working with Words

Here are some questions to ask yourself to determine how well you are doing Working with Words and to help you grow in this block.

_____ **1.** Am I limiting the number of Word Wall words and including words that are high frequency and/or have useful spelling patterns?

_____ **2.** Am I displaying the words on colorful paper, under the letters they begin with, big enough for students to see, and in a place where everyone can easily see them?

_____ **3.** Am I doing a daily practice in which the class and I chant and write five words, and am I emphasizing handwriting as we write the words?

_____ **4.** Once students can chant and write the words quickly, am I including some On-the-Back activities that help them learn the words and apply the patterns to other words?

_____ **5.** Once words are on the Word Wall, do I hold students accountable for spelling the words correctly in everything they write?

_____ **6.** Am I including a variety of activities (Making Words, Rounding Up the Rhymes, Guess the Covered Word, etc.) to help students learn to decode and spell using patterns?

_____ **7.** Am I emphasizing the transfer of Working with Words activities to actually decoding words while reading and spelling words while writing (for example, including all three steps—make, sort, and transfer—in my Making Words lessons)?

_____ **8.** Am I keeping a brisk pace with my Working with Words activities so that I can complete them in 20 minutes, have time to emphasize transfer, and keep students engaged?

_____ **9.** Do I remind students when they are actually reading and writing during the other three blocks to use the strategies we practice during Working with Words activities?

_____ **10.** On some days, do I connect my Working with Words activities to something read aloud or during Guided Reading or to my science and social studies topics?

_____ **11.** Do I display a chart of theme, unit, or monthly words to support students' writing without cluttering up the Word Wall?

_____ **12.** Am I pacing this block so that it is completed in 30 minutes?

Making the Working with Words Block Multilevel

All of the activities in the Working with Words Block are inherently multilevel. Here is a description of how each activity benefits students of all abilities within a classroom.

Word Walls

Someone watching students doing the daily Word Wall practice might assume that they are all learning the same thing—how to spell words. What they are doing externally, however, may not reveal what they are processing internally.

Imagine that the five new words added to the wall one week are **come**, **make**, **they**, **boy**, and **where**. During the daily Word Wall practice, students who have already learned to read them are learning to spell them. Other students, however, who require a lot of practice with words are learning to read them. Still other students are learning to use these words to read and spell a lot of other words (for example: **toy**, **cake**, **fake**, **flake**, **shake**, **snake**, etc.).

Rounding Up the Rhymes

While Rounding Up the Rhymes, some students are still developing their phonemic awareness as they decide which words rhyme, and they are learning that rhyming words usually—but not always—have the same spelling pattern. As they use the words rounded up to read and spell new words, students who need it are getting practice with beginning-letter substitution. Students who already have well-developed phonemic awareness and beginning-letter knowledge are practicing the important strategy of using known words to decode and spell unknown rhyming words.

Making Words

Making Words lessons are multilevel in a number of ways. Each lesson begins with short, easy words and progresses to medium-size and big words. Every Making Words lesson ends with the teacher asking, "Has anyone figured out the word we can make if we use all of our letters?" Figuring out the secret word that can be made from all of the letters in the limited time is a challenge to even the most advanced readers. Making Words also includes students with very limited literacy, who enjoy manipulating the letters and making the words even if they don't get them completed until the word is made in the pocket chart. Ending each lesson by sorting the words into patterns and using those patterns to read and spell some new words helps students of all levels see how to use the patterns in words to read and spell other words.

Guess the Covered Word

Guess the Covered Word lessons provide review for beginning-letter sounds for those who still need it. The most sophisticated readers are consolidating the important strategies of using meaning, beginning letters, and word length as clues to identifying an unknown word.

Using Words You Know

Using Words You Know lessons provide students who still need it with a lot of practice with rhyming words and with the idea that spelling pattern and rhyme are connected. Depending on what they already know, some students realize how words they know can help them decode while other students realize how these words help them spell. To make the lesson a bit more multilevel at the upper end, include a few longer words that rhyme and help students see how their known words can help them spell the rhyming part of longer words.

Reading/Writing Rhymes

Reading/Writing Rhymes is perhaps the most multilevel activity. All beginning letters, including the common single consonants and the less-common, more-complex digraphs and blends, are reviewed each time you distribute the onset cards. Phonemic awareness is developed as students say all of the rhyming words and blend the vowel patterns with the beginning letters. Students whose word awareness is more sophisticated learn that there are often two spellings for the long vowel patterns and develop their visual checking sense as they see the rhyming words with the different patterns written on the same chart. They also learn the correct spellings for many common homophones. The addition of some longer rhyming words helps them learn how to decode and spell longer words and allows them to write more interesting rhymes.

The Guided Reading Block

30-40 min.

GOALS

- To teach comprehension skills and strategies
- To develop students' background knowledge, meaningful vocabulary, and oral language
- To teach students how to read all types of literature
- To provide as much instructional-level reading as possible
- To maintain the motivation and self-confidence of struggling readers

Depending on the time of year, the needs of the class, the personality of the teacher, and the dictates of the school or school system, Guided Reading is carried out with the adopted basal reader, basal readers from previously adopted series, multiple copies of trade books, big books, or various combinations of these. **The purposes of this block are to expose students to a wide range of literature, to teach comprehension strategies, and to teach students how to read material that becomes increasingly harder.** When using basal readers, you should pick and choose activities. In the Guided Reading Block, select activities that focus on comprehension.

Try to provide as much instructional-level reading as possible during this block. Students are not reading at their levels during Guided Reading every day.

- Students who read well above grade level profit from the comprehension instruction and a balanced diet of different types of reading, but they do most of their on-level reading during Self-Selected Reading.

- Students who read below grade level are provided strong support when grade-level materials are being read, and they have opportunities for as much easy reading as possible. Many struggling readers, however, do most of their on-level reading during Self-Selected Reading and when teachers put students in small, flexible reading groups.

If Guided Reading were the only block taught consistently in the classroom, it could not be organized as it is, but the other three blocks—Self-Selected Reading, Writing, and Working with Words—provide numerous appropriate reading and writing opportunities for above- and below-level readers.

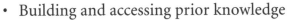

Guided Reading lessons usually have a before-reading phase, a during-reading phase, and an after-reading phase. Depending on the text being read, the comprehension strategies being taught, and the reading levels of students, there can be a great variety of before-, during-, and after-reading variations.

Before students read, help them with the following:

- Building and accessing prior knowledge
- Making connections to personal experiences
- Developing vocabulary essential for comprehension
- Taking a picture walk
- Making predictions
- Setting purposes for their reading
- Starting a graphic organizer or KWL chart

You may use the following variations during reading:

- Choral reading
- Echo reading
- Shared reading
- Partner reading
- Reading teams
- Coaching groups
- Three-Ring Circus (alone, with partners, or with you)
- Book Club groups
- Everyone Read To . . . (ERT)
- Sticky note reading

After reading, help students with the following:

- Discussing what they read
- Connecting new knowledge to what they already know
- Following up predictions
- Acting out the story
- Discussing what they have learned and how they are becoming better readers by using the reading strategies
- Completing the graphic organizer or KWL chart

The Guided Reading Block

Guided Reading in the primary grades usually includes several readings of each selection.

- **Instead of always first reading the selection to students, teachers often begin Guided Reading with a picture walk through the book.** They lead students to name the things in the pictures and make predictions, and they point out a few critical vocabulary words with which students might have difficulty as they read the selection.

- **Students then read the selection individually, with partners, or in small, flexible groups with the teacher.** The class reconvenes, discusses the selection, and may read it again in some other format (not round-robin, however!). Comprehension strategies are taught and practiced. Predictions made before reading are checked. Story maps and webs are completed.

- **The next reading of the selection might include a writing activity.** This writing activity is also done by some students individually, some with partners, and others in a group guided by the teacher.

- **Often, the final reading is a dramatization of the selection** with various students playing different parts as the rest of the class reads or tells the story.

Use a variety of whole-class, small-group, partner, and individual formats as your class reads and rereads selections. Along with deciding how to have students read a selection, decide what can be done before and after reading to promote comprehension. The next two sections describe some of the most commonly used before-, during-, and after-reading variations.

Reading Variations

Choral Reading

Choral reading works best for poetry, refrains, and books with a lot of conversation. The whole class can read, the girls and boys can alternate reading, or rows or tables can alternate. Old favorites, such as "The Itsy Bitsy Spider," "Five Little Pumpkins," "Rudolph the Red-Nosed Reindeer," "Here Comes Peter Cottontail," poetry, nursery rhymes, and finger plays are naturals for choral reading. Choral reading is also a wonderful way to reread books, such as *The Lion and the Mouse* by Cheyenne Cisco, in which the two main characters talk to each other.

Echo Reading

In echo reading, the teacher reads first and students become the echo, reading the lines back. As students echo read, they try to match the teacher's emphasis and fluency. Echo reading is usually done one sentence at a time, and it is most effective when there are different voices and relatively short sentences. *I Went Walking* by Sue Williams and *Hattie and the Fox* by Mem Fox are favorites for easy echo reading.

Shared Reading

One important kind of guided reading in the primary grades is shared reading with predictable big books. **Predictable books are books with repeated patterns of refrains, pictures, or rhymes. Shared reading with big books is an extension of the "lap experience" that we wish all students had had at home before beginning school, in which children were read to while sitting on someone's lap or snuggled close to someone.** Being read to in this way gave each child an opportunity to look at pictures and print up close and to ask questions about the book. Children often asked for the same book to be read over and over. In shared reading with big books, students can see both the pictures and the print as the teacher reads. Just like at home, one reading is never enough! *Brown Bear, Brown Bear, What Do You See?* by Bill Martin Jr. and *Mrs. Wishy Washy* by Joy Cowley are common books for shared reading.

Comprehension activities often include the following:

The class might "do the book," with some students assuming roles and becoming the characters as the rest of the students read the book. Little books based on the big books are read and reread with partners and then read individually or in small groups. Class books and take-home books patterned on the big book are often constructed in shared writing activities.

The big books read during Guided Reading are sometimes chosen because they fit a theme or unit that the class is studying. On these days, Guided Reading time flows seamlessly into other unit-oriented activities.

Even when students have begun to read and develop their reading strategies, they can still benefit from the shared reading of big books. Shared reading provides an opportunity for the teacher to model a strategy as all students watch. Of course, the big books used with more accomplished readers have more text and are less predictable than the big books used with emergent readers.

Here is an example using *The Lion and the Mouse* by Cheyenne Cisco. This is a great book for helping students develop a better understanding of characters, conversation, and quotation marks. This fable has two contrasting animals in it: a big, bossy lion and a quiet, little mouse.

The shared reading begins with a picture walk. The teacher and students talk about what they see in the pictures. The teacher leads students to talk about how fierce the lion looks and how he roars when he talks. Next, a quiet, little mouse comes along and tries to pick a berry from a bush. As the mouse creeps closer, the lion wakes up and catches the mouse by the tail. The mouse looks like he is begging for the lion to spare his life. It looks as if the lion will eat the mouse, but on the next page, the mouse is running away. Later, the lion is caught in a rope and the mouse is listening to his roars.

Before turning the page, the teacher asks, "How many of you think that the mouse will help the lion? How many of you think that the mouse won't help the lion? How could the mouse help the lion?"

They turn the page and see a picture of the mouse chewing the rope and the lion walking away. Students comment that on the last pages the lion and mouse look like friends. The teacher asks, "What do you think they are saying to each other?"

Next, the teacher says, "Listen as I read *The Lion and the Mouse.* The two characters talk a lot in this book. Listen to how different the lion's and the mouse's voices are when they talk and see if you can find what the mouse says to keep the lion from eating him."

Then, the teacher reads the book. She uses a big, deep voice for the lion and a little whisper voice for the mouse.

At the end of the story, the teacher asks students, "How does the lion sound when he talks? How does the mouse sound when he talks? What does the mouse say to stop the lion from eating him?"

Students discuss the different voices of the lion and mouse and explain that the mouse keeps the lion from eating him by promising to help the lion someday. The teacher and the class discuss how the mouse helps the lion and whether a mouse and lion could really be friends.

For the second reading of the book, the teacher comments that the first page has no quotation marks but that the second page does. A student is asked to come up and show which words are in quotation marks. Then, the teacher reads each page and asks students to listen to determine who is saying the words in quotation marks. After each page is read, students decide that the lion is talking, and together, they read just the words that the lion says.

For the next page, the teacher asks students if they see any quotation marks. They don't see any, so they decide that no one is talking on this page. The teacher reads the page to them, and they go on to the next page. Here, they find some quotation marks. A student comes up and points to the words in quotation marks. The teacher reads as students listen for who is talking and what is said. Then, with the teacher, students read just what is said, using the appropriate loud or quiet voice. They finish the second reading of the book in this way.

For the third reading, the teacher chooses a choral-reading format. The class is divided in half into "lions" and "mice." The teacher reads all of the words that are not in quotation marks. Students read their animal parts, roaring or whispering. After this third reading, they discuss how the lion and mouse sound different depending on what is happening in the story.

Since all of the "mice" want to be "lions," the class reads the story one more time with students trading roles.

The teacher ends the shared-reading activity by having students explain how quotation marks are used and how the characters change during the story.

The next day, the teacher gathers students together and reminds them that yesterday, they talked about how different the lion and mouse are. The teacher then asks them to listen for opposites as she reads the first two pages of the book. Students identify the opposites **big** and **little** and **quiet** and **noisy.** The teacher writes these on an opposites chart. They read the next two pages together and identify **yelled/shouted** and **whispered,** which the teacher adds to the chart.

The teacher then explains that students will read the little book versions of the big book in groups of three and that they will read it three times. For the first reading, one student is the lion, one is the mouse, and one is the narrator. They will switch parts for the next two readings so that each student reads each part. When students finish reading, they write down more opposites to add to the chart.

Benefits of Shared Reading

Shared reading provides opportunities for teachers to model for students how to think as they read. By using big books in which students can see the print and pictures, teachers can focus students' attention on whatever strategy is being developed. Shared reading of big books should not be confined to kindergarten and early first grade. Rather, teachers should find and use big books that help them demonstrate by "thinking aloud" when new comprehension strategies are being introduced.

During shared reading, there are many different things that can be learned, depending on what students are ready to learn. Students who have had little experience with reading learn how print works, how to track print, and how the pictures and words support each other. They learn a few words and learn how noticing the letters helps them tell which word is which. For students who are further along in reading, shared reading provides opportunities to learn many words. All students enjoy shared reading, and participating in shared-reading lessons helps them build concepts, vocabulary, and comprehension strategies. There is something for everyone in a good shared-reading lesson, and consequently, shared reading is one of the most multilevel formats.

Partner Reading

Students accept the fact that some of their friends are better dancers or artists. In real life, friends often learn from and help each other. **Partner reading allows friends to help each other read, just as they help each other with other activities.**

For partner reading to be effective, students need to learn a variety of ways to do it.

- Some days are designated as "take turns" days, when partners take turns reading the pages and helping each other as needed.

- On other days that are designated as "ask questions" days, partners read each page silently and ask each other questions about the page before going on to the next page.

- On "sticky note" days, partners are given sticky notes to mark things they want to remember. They have a limited number of sticky notes and must decide together where to put the notes to mark what they find to be most interesting, important, or confusing.

- Occasionally, the teacher declares a "you decide" day on which partners can decide to read together in any method they wish.

Having these different kinds of partner-reading formats provides some variety in the reading. It also ensures that students engage in both silent and oral reading.

Assigning Partners

There are a variety of ways to assign partners. **Generally, you should pair students who work well together.** It would be ideal to pair a student who is struggling with a student who can help—and who will help nicely. A partner who belittles a struggling reader will not provide the kind of support and confidence-building that is needed.

Some teachers use stickers in different colors and shapes to designate partners and to determine who will read first. Imagine that you have a selection that many students in your class will need support to read. You want all students who may need help to have a partner who will help nicely. You also want the better readers to read the first two-page spread, in which many of the names and other important vocabulary words are used.

1. Consider whom you will pair with whom, pairing the most struggling readers with your most considerate and nurturing, better readers.

2. Give the stronger reader in one pair a blue square and give the other student a blue circle. Continue with other colors until all pairs have stickers in each shape.

3. When it is time to read, simply have students find partners with the same color stickers and tell them that squares read first today.

4. All partners who cooperate well, help each other, and use quiet voices get to keep their stickers.

Teacher's Role

When all students are reading with partners, the teacher circulates through the classroom, listening to them read, helping if needed, and making anecdotal notes. These notes should be about students' reading fluency, their discussion, how they are figuring out words, and how they are helping each other. By stopping for just a minute and listening to each set of partners, you can monitor all students' reading in a 12- to 15-minute period.

Reading Teams

The guidelines for partner reading also apply to reading teams. Think about whom to assign to which groups, how long to leave the groups together, where they will meet, and any other logistical variables. Reading teams should know what format they will use, and they can use all formats described for partnerships—and a few others. They should know what their purpose is, how long they have, and what they should do if they finish before time is up. In the beginning, the teacher circulates, commenting and making notes on how the groups are functioning. Once students know how to work in reading teams, the teacher's focus shifts to noticing how individual students are doing.

Because reading teams have many students, this is the format to use when doing any of the "doing the book" activities. You may also do small-group discussions in reading teams. After doing a graphic organizer or KWL chart several times as a whole-class activity, you may turn the activity over to the reading teams. Students can contribute ideas, and one student can write on the chart. Finally, all charts are compared and displayed.

Each reading team always has a "coach," and every student should have chances to be the coach. Not everyone will get to be the coach the same number of times, but the same "bossy" students cannot be the coaches every time!

To get around this problem, consider which reading-team formats do not require a super reader. Imagine that the class has read a story and done an appropriate activity with it the preceding day. Today, they will need to reread the story to decide what the characters are saying and doing on each page in preparation for pantomiming the book. Divide your struggling readers and make each a coach in a group. The rest of the group will take turns reading the pages. Since you read it the day before and the struggling readers are not reading aloud, the other students should be able to fluently read their pages aloud. The coach tells everyone whose turn it is and asks, "Who is talking, and how would they act?"

Each struggling reader can also be a coach when the format being used by the reading team is choral reading. For echo reading, on the other hand, you need one of the best readers to be the coach. If the groups are doing a "talking why and how" discussion, your struggling readers might be the coaches because the coaches are leading the discussions while others read the questions and talk about what they think are the answers. When groups do Everyone Read To . . . , they need good readers to formulate the purposes for reading each page.

Reading teams is one of students' favorite formats for reading and rereading selections. With some clever thinking, you can allow all students to be coaches on various days. As students read, you can circulate and coach them as they need help with words or with the thinking required to fulfill their purpose(s) for reading. In addition to coaching students as they circulate around the room, some teachers like to appoint a word coach in each group. This is the only person in the group who can help someone figure out a word. The word coach and the main coach are not the same person, so this gives you more opportunities to let students who are not the best readers be the coaches.

Coaching Groups: Small, Flexible Groups

Often, the teacher meets with a small, flexible group of students to coach them as they are reading. Students in this group participate in the before- and after-reading activities with the whole class; this coaching group is how you help students apply the strategies that they have been learning. When reading with the small group, try to avoid having students take turns. Students should read softly but still loudly enough for you to hear so that you can coach them when they need help.

Before students start to read, remind them of the strategies that they can use to figure out an unfamiliar word.

1. Put your finger on the unknown word and say all of the letters.

2. Use the letters and the picture clues.

3. Try to pronounce the word by looking to see if it has a spelling pattern that you know.

4. Keep your finger on the word and read the rest of the sentence to see if what you think the word is makes sense.

5. If it doesn't make sense, go back to the word in the sentence and try to think of what would make sense and contain those letters.

When a student is stumped by a word while reading, prompt him to use these strategies by giving clues, such as the following:

- "Yes, this word is spelled **g-r-u-m-p**. We have a word on our Word Wall spelled **j-u-m-p**."

- "Do you see an animal in the picture that might be spelled **d-r-a-g-o-n**?"

- "What could you use to dig a hole that begins with the sound **/sh/**?"

Once the student has figured out a word, remind him to go back and reread the sentence to see if it sounds right.

Teachers call together coaching groups for a variety of reasons. Students who need a lot of support are included in these groups more often than accelerated readers, but these groups are *not* ability-based groups. The members of the groups change each time a coaching group is called, and the teacher should include some able readers to model good reading strategies.

Three-Ring Circus

On some days, the teacher may want certain students to read the selection on their own and others to read it with partners while the teacher meets with a small coaching group. This Three-Ring Circus is not as difficult to achieve as might be expected.

1. First, explain to students that there are advantages to all three types of reading. When they are reading by themselves, they can read at their own paces and focus on their own ideas. When they are partner reading, they have the advantage of getting help when they need it, and they have someone with whom to share ideas. Explain to students that you like to read with a small group so that you can see how students are progressing and help them apply the strategies that they are learning.

2. Second, make sure that students know how to read with their partners and what kind of partner format you want them to use on this particular day.

3. Finally, you need an organizational chart so that students can quickly see how they will read the selection that day and not waste time waiting for you to get everyone in the right place. Below is a Three-Ring Circus chart that one teacher uses to let students know how they will be reading. On days when the teacher wants to have a Three-Ring Circus organization, she places students' names in the appropriate rings.

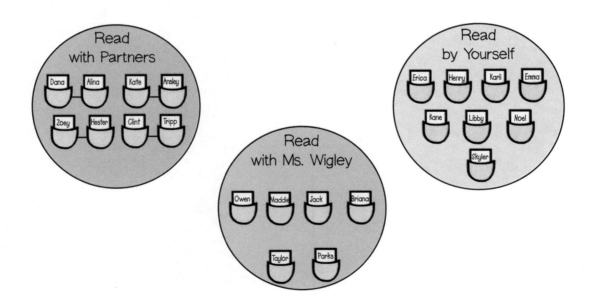

The Guided Reading Block

When planning a Three-Ring Circus, consider the levels of students and the reading selection when deciding which method each student should use for reading. Accelerated readers often read the selection individually or with partners of similar ability. Students who need support are paired with supportive partners or assigned to the coaching group. Do not assign pairs who do not work well together and never assign a student to read individually unless she can successfully complete the reading alone.

Book Club Groups

For Book Club groups, the teacher selects three or four books that are tied together by author, genre, topic, or theme. After reading aloud the first several pages or chapter of each book, or previewing the pictures with students, the teacher asks students to indicate their first and second choices (and third choices, if there are four books) for which books they would like to read.

When choosing the books for Book Club groups, try to include one that is easier and one that is harder. If students who are struggling list the easier book as one of their choices, put them in the group that will read this book. If the advanced readers list the harder book as one of their choices, put them in the group that will read the harder book. (Don't tell students that some books are easier or harder!) Each time a class does Book Club groups, students are placed in different groups. While the reading levels and choices of students are considered when assigning groups, each group has a range of readers and is not ability based.

Once Book Club groups are formed, they meet regularly to read and discuss books. The teacher rotates through the groups, giving guidance, support, and encouragement. Each day, the groups report to the whole class what has happened or what they have learned in their books.

Here is an example using four informational books: *Cats, Wolves, Sharks,* and *Sea Turtles,* all by Gail Gibbons. Because a familiar topic for most students is cats and because there is less text on each page, *Cats* is an easier book than the other three. *Sea Turtles* is a little harder than *Wolves* or *Sharks.*

The teacher begins Guided Reading today by telling students that he has found four wonderful informational animal books. One at a time, he shows the covers of the books. He lets students tell what they know about each of the four animals and share some of their personal experiences with the other students. Using only the covers, he gets students to think about what they know and what they might learn. Then, he tells students that they have only this week to spend on these books and that the class has only seven copies of each book. Not everyone will be able to read all four books, but they will read one book in their Book Club group and hear about the animals in the books that the other groups are reading.

Next, the teacher gives each student an index card. He asks students to write their names and the numbers 1, 2, and 3 on the cards. He explains that they will have 20 minutes to preview the books—five minutes for each book. At the end of the 20 minutes, they will return to their seats and write down their first, second, and third choices.

He places all copies of each book in four separate areas. Then, he divides the class into four random groups and sends a group to each area. He sets a timer for five minutes and tells students that when the timer sounds, they must move to the next area and the next group of books.

For the next 20 minutes, students try to read and look at as many pages as they can. Each time the timer sounds and they have to move to the next area, students may complain that they haven't had enough time. The teacher sympathizes but tells them that this time is not for studying the books; it is only to decide which book they most want to read.

When the 20 minutes are up, students return to their seats to make their choices. It isn't easy! Most protest that they want to read all four books. They have trouble deciding which are their first choices and which are their second choices. The teacher tells them not to worry too much about the order of choices because he can't guarantee that they will get their first choices—or even their second choices. There are only seven copies of each book, and the groups should be about the same size.

After school, the teacher looks at the cards. First, he looks at the cards of the struggling readers. Four of his five struggling readers have listed *Cats* as one of their choices, so he puts them along with three more capable readers who have also chosen *Cats*, in the *Cats* group. One struggling reader chose *Sharks* as her first choice, so the teacher puts her in the *Sharks* group.

Next, the teacher looks at the choices of his strongest readers. Five of these students have chosen *Sea Turtles*, and he puts them, along with one fairly fluent reader, in the *Sea Turtles* group. He puts the other students in groups according to their choices and evens out the numbers.

He takes four sheets of chart paper and heads each with the name of a book and the names of the students in that group. He then divides each chart into three columns and heads them **K**, **W**, and **L**. (See pages 69–70 for a more detailed explanation of KWL charts.) He chooses one student in each group to be the leader and do the recording, and he places a star by that student's name. He places the charts and the books in the four reading areas. Using a large paper clip, he clips together the pages in the last two-thirds of each book so that students will not read beyond the first 10 pages on the first day.

When students come into the classroom the next morning, they immediately find their names on the charts and know which books they will read. Some are disappointed that they didn't get their first choices. The teacher sympathizes but points out that the books will be available during Self-Selected Reading next week.

At Guided Reading time, the groups go to their areas and the teacher explains how they will work for the next three days. He has done many KWL charts with them, so they know that they brainstorm things they **K**now for the first column and things they **W**ant to learn for the second column. He gives a marker to the leader of each group. He tells students that the leader will be the "teacher" and lead the group just as he does when the class does KWL charts together.

The teacher asks the groups to spend 10 minutes putting things they know and want to learn in the first two columns. He sets the timer for 10 minutes and circulates among the groups, encouraging each group to list as much as they can in the first two columns. When the timer sounds, he tells them to finish writing and begin reading the book.

The teacher explains that they will now have 20 minutes to read the pages in the first third of the book and add things to the **L**earned column on the chart. They will read each two-page spread silently or using whisper voices, and then list things in the **L** column before going to the next two-page spread.

As the groups work, the teacher helps them decide what to write and reminds them how he writes the information when they do KWL charts as a class. He begins with the *Cats* group and spends more time here. Even though there are three pretty good readers in this group, the four struggling readers need support and encouragement. The teacher does, of course, make sure that the leader and teacher in this group is one of the more-advanced readers and writers.

At the end of 19 minutes, the teacher signals that the groups have one minute remaining and that they should finish writing on the charts. One group has not gotten to the last two-page spread. The teacher tells them that tomorrow they can begin there and will need to move a little faster.

The last 10 minutes are spent with each group sharing what they have learned so far with the rest of the class.

For the next two days, the groups review what they have learned, add a few more questions to the **W** column, read the final two-thirds of the book, and add to the **L** column. Each day ends with the groups sharing what they have learned.

On the fifth day, the groups reassemble for the last time. Their task today is to read everything they have listed in the **L** column. Then, each student writes the three most interesting things that she has learned and draws a picture to illustrate the new knowledge. The teacher gives students a paragraph frame like the one on the following page to organize their writing.

> I learned a lot about _____. I learned
> that _____. I also learned that
> _____. The most interesting thing that
> I learned was _____.

Students work busily to write and illustrate their paragraphs using both the books and the KWL charts. All students write good paragraphs since they know so much about their topics, have the books and KWL charts for support, and use the paragraph frame to help structure their writing.

Miguel

I learned a lot about cats. I learned that baby cats are called kittens. I learned that cats are good pets. The most interesting thing I learned was that cats are good hunters.

Ashley

I learned a lot about sea turtles. I learned that they live in warm waters. I also learned that turtles lived 200 million years ago. The most interesting thing I learned was the leatherback sea turtle is 7 feet long and it weighs 1,000 pounds.

Jared

I learned a lot about wolves. I learned that some wolves can run up to 40 mph. I also learned that most male wolves weigh over 100 pounds. The most interesting thing I learned was that wolves can talk to each other.

Book Club groups are a great way to organize Guided Reading once students read well enough that the teacher can find multiple books tied together in some way. It is also crucial that the teacher has modeled the formats that the groups will use (in this example, KWL charts and paragraph frames). Most teachers find that students participate eagerly in their Book Club groups and that the books they didn't get to read are the most popular selections during Self-Selected Reading the following week. It is not unusual for students to read all three books that their group didn't read. Because each group shares information about their book, students' knowledge of each book is greatly increased, and they are often able to read books at higher levels than usual.

Everyone Read To . . . (ERT)

Everyone Read To . . . (ERT) is a way of guiding the whole class or a small group through the reading of a selection. Teachers use ERT when they want students to do the initial reading on their own, but when they also want to keep students together so that they can provide guidance and support for the initial reading. **Through this method, the teacher tells students to read to either "find" or "figure out." They read the segment, and then the teacher follows up on whatever purpose was set by asking questions, such as the following:**

- "What was making the sky so dark?"
- "What new things did you learn?"
- "What seems to be the problem in this story?"
- "Who figured out what kind of class Miss Nelson has?"

When the information for which students are reading is stated directly on the page, the teacher asks them to read to **find**. When they have to make inferences, the teacher asks students to read to **figure out**.

Students tell in their own words what they read, and everyone goes on to the next segment. For older students, Everyone Read To . . . is usually silent reading. Because students must develop some reading fluency before they can "read it in their minds," this ERT time with young students is often not silent but rather whisper reading. In ERT, everyone reads the text for himself in whatever way is appropriate to find specific information he will then share with the class. Here is an ERT example using the book *Three Cheers for Tacky* by Helen Lester.

The teacher and students have read the title and the author's and illustrator's names, and they have taken a picture walk through the book. They will now do the first reading of the book, and the teacher will guide them through each two-page spread, using ERT to help them set a purpose.

For the first page, the teacher reminds students that during their picture walk, they decided that the penguins are the main characters in the story and that one penguin is always doing things differently from the other five. She says, "Everybody read this page to **find** more about our penguin characters."

Students read the page to themselves, some without any lip movement and others whisper reading it. As they finish, students raise their hands, and the teacher calls on them to tell her what they found out about the penguin characters.

Different students add information until all of the relevant facts on the page are given. Students have learned that the penguins are named Goodly, Lovely, Angel, Neatly, Perfect, and Tacky. Tacky is the different one. The teacher and students repeat the names of the five "normal" penguins and the name of the "odd" bird, Tacky. Students enjoy the names and talk about how the author lets you know right away that Tacky will not act, look, or dress like the other five penguins in the story.

They turn the page, and the teacher reminds students that during their picture walk, they concluded from the pictures that the penguins are in school. Now, she says, "Everyone read to **find** what these penguins do in their school and what Tacky does that is different."

Again, students read silently or quietly. Raised hands let the teacher know when students are ready to discuss what they have read.

They turn the page again, and the teacher reminds students that they read the sign in the picture ("GREAT PENGUIN CHEERING CONTEST") during their picture walk. Students also talk about how the little picture above each penguin probably indicates how the penguins imagine they would look in the cheering contest. Students read to **find** what the penguins are planning for their parts in the cheering contest.

The teacher leads the class through each two-page spread in this manner. For each spread, she reminds students of what they learned from the pictures and sets a purpose for the page that seems to be what someone would want to find after having pondered the pictures:

- "Everyone read to find what words they are cheering as they do each of these actions."

- "Everyone read to find how Tacky does the cheer."

- "Everyone read to find what the other five penguins tell Tacky he has to do if he will be on their team."

- "Everyone read to figure out why Tacky is dressed in those funny clothes."

- "Everyone read to figure out if Tacky will ever be able to do the cheer."

The reading of the story continues in this way, and students enjoy the story. Thinking about what they see in the pictures helps students figure out what the words might say and gives them an idea of what to read for. Reading to **find** is literal comprehension. Reading to **figure out** is inferential.

The teacher concludes the lesson by telling students that this is a book that "just demands to be acted out" and that they will act it out tomorrow. They quickly look through the pages of the book again and begin to make some plans for tomorrow. The teacher helps them by asking questions, such as the following:

- "What characters will we need for this page?"

- "What will they do?"

- "What will they say?"

- "How will they look?"

Students begin to talk about which characters they want to be. The teacher says that there will be different casts for different pages and that students will play many different parts as the entire book is reenacted.

Sticky Note Reading

Sticky note reading can be done by students reading alone, with partners, in small groups, or by the whole class. Students use sticky notes to mark what they find interesting, important, or confusing. Sticky notes work particularly well when students have made predictions or have begun a KWL chart or graphic organizer before reading. As students find something in their reading that proves or disproves a prediction or needs to be added to the KWL chart or graphic organizer, they write a word or phrase on the sticky note and place it next to where they found the information. During any follow-up activities, students can refer to their notes and sometimes read aloud the related information.

Sticky notes can also be used for writing a word that the reader couldn't pronounce or for which he didn't know the meaning. Again, the sticky note is placed next to the troublesome word so that when the student tells the word, the sentence in which it occurred can be found easily. The teacher and the other students can then help the student figure out the pronunciation or meaning.

Once students know how to use sticky notes to mark information and troublesome words, you may combine the two by giving them two colors of sticky notes. For example, students might use yellow sticky notes to mark words or phrases that give information and pink sticky notes for confusing words.

Students have much more to add to the after-reading discussions when they marked information with sticky notes as they encountered it. They monitor their own comprehension better if they have other sticky notes to mark troublesome words. Students also enjoy reading more because adding colorful sticky notes to pages is fun!

Before- and After-Reading Variations

Picture Walks

Before reading, the teacher and students take a picture walk through the book. The teacher helps students use the pictures to build important concepts by asking questions, such as the following:

- "Do you know what this is called?"

- "What does it look like he is doing here?"

- "What holiday does it look like they are celebrating?"

Based on students' responses, the teacher confirms their ideas and/or suggests words and phrases.

- "We can call it a hatchet. We can also call it an ax. Have you ever heard someone say that they chopped wood with an ax?"

- "Yes, it looks like he is fixing a flat tire. He uses the jack to hold up the car."

- "Yes, they are having Thanksgiving dinner."

Once the targeted word has been used by students or suggested by the teacher, the teacher sometimes leads students to look at the print on the page and to find a word that would be especially difficult for them to decode on their own:

"Let's say **Thanksgiving** together. **Thanksgiving.** Will the word **Thanksgiving** be a short word or a long word? Yes, **Thanksgiving** will be a long word. With what two letters do you think **Thanksgiving** might begin? Say **Thanksgiving** again. What three letters do you expect to see at the end of **Thanksgiving**? Now, look at the print and put your finger on a word that might be **Thanksgiving**."

The picture walk should be brief but should help students use the pictures to connect to their own experiences and anticipate what they will be reading. Teachers can also help students develop vocabulary by using some new words and by connecting these words to the pictures. Students can be led to identify some words in the text that might be impossible for most of them to figure out if they encountered them on their own.

Predictions

A time-tested way to help students access prior knowledge and connect reading to experience and to engage them while reading is to have them make predictions before they begin reading.

1. Many teachers read just the first page or two of a story aloud to students. Then, they ask, "What do you think will happen?"

2. All responses are accepted and followed by a question to evoke student thinking: "What makes you think that?"

3. The teacher is nonjudgmental and says something like, "That's an interesting idea. I never thought of that. She could do that, couldn't she?"

Teachers may record predictions on a chart, writing the initials of the student who made each prediction.

Helping students make predictions before they read is a powerful strategy. Instead of the teacher setting a purpose and telling students what information to look for as they read, students learn to set their own purposes. This is what "real" readers do. They begin making predictions from the moment they see the title and cover of a book. As they read the first several pages, they think ahead about what may happen. Sometimes, a prediction is very specific ("If he takes that job working after school, he'll never have time to practice for the basketball tryouts!"). Other times, a prediction is more general ("Uh, oh! There will be trouble here!").

Predictions sometimes prove true, while at other times, the reader is surprised. When helping students make predictions, don't emphasize whether the predictions are right or wrong. Rather, put the emphasis on the predictions making sense. Sometimes, you may even tell students that their predictions were wonderful and that the author may have written a more interesting story if she had used the plot they predicted!

The importance of predictions is not whether they are right or wrong but that they are made. Once students have made predictions, their attention is engaged and their comprehension is enhanced. Teachers produce motivated, active, engaged readers when they regularly help students make predictions based on the cover, title, first few pages, and illustrations of a book and follow the reading by discussing which predictions really happen and what surprises the author had in store.

KWL Charts

Perhaps the most effective and popular way of helping students access prior knowledge and make predictions for informational text is the KWL chart (Ogle, 1986; Carr and Ogle, 1987). The letters stand for what students **K**now, what they **W**ant to learn, and what they have **L**earned. Here is an example of a KWL chart using *Animal Tracks* by Arthur Dorros.

The lesson begins with the teacher directing students' attention to the pictures of animals and tracks on the cover of the book. He asks students what they know about tracks. Students respond that they have seen animal tracks in the snow, on a dry sidewalk, or after the dog walks into the house with dirty paws!

On a large piece of chart paper, the teacher has labeled three columns **K**, **W**, and **L**. He writes what students know under the **K** column. They know that birds leave tracks, and so do animals and people. They know that the tracks are made by the animals' feet or paws. They know that animals leave different kinds of tracks depending on their feet. The know that big animals leave big tracks and that small animals leave small tracks.

Next, the teacher asks students what they want to learn about animal tracks. One student wants to know if all animals leave tracks. Another student wants to know how people can tell which animal has left the tracks. The teacher writes these two questions in the **W** column.

KWL		
Know	**W**ant to Learn	**L**earned
Birds make tracks.	Do all animals make tracks?	
Animals make tracks.	How can you tell which animal has left the tracks?	
People can make tracks.		
Tracks are made by the feet or paws of animals.		
Different animals leave different kinds of tracks.		
Big animals make big tracks.		
Small animals make small tracks.		

The teacher tells the class that today they will read *Animal Tracks* with partners to find out if their two questions are answered in the book and to find out what other new things they can add to the **L** column. If they finish reading before the time is up, they should discuss the answers to the two questions and write down things to add to the **L** column.

The teacher explains that *Animal Tracks* is kind of like a puzzle book. Each page ends with a question about who made the tracks. The question is answered on the next page. He tells students to try to answer the question before turning the page. He calls out the names of students who will be partners and reminds them to read in whisper voices. He reminds the partners to help each other figure out words rather than just telling what the words are.

When students finish reading, the teacher calls them all together to complete the last column. Students list the new information they have learned, and the teacher records it on the chart.

Whatever the teacher does before reading to set up comprehension must be followed up after reading. Here is the KWL chart that one class completed together after reading:

KWL

<u>Know</u>	<u>Want to Learn</u>	<u>Learned</u>
Birds make tracks.	Do all animals make tracks?	All animals that walk can make tracks.
Animals make tracks.	How can you tell which animal has left the tracks?	You can tell what animal made the tracks because the tracks look like the animal's feet.
People can make tracks.		
Tracks are made by the feet or paws of animals.		There needs to be water or soft ground to see tracks.
Different animals leave different kinds of tracks.		
Big animals make big tracks.		
Small animals make small tracks.		

Graphic Organizers

Another popular before-reading strategy for informational text is to start a web, a data chart, or another graphic organizer. **To decide which graphic organizer to use, read the book and determine what the important information is and how the information can best be organized and displayed.**

Many informational texts lend themselves to several different graphic organizers. The following examples are based on the book *Wonderful Worms* by Linda Glaser.

Web

Looking through this book, the teacher notices important information about earthworms: what they look like, where they live, how they dig, how they move, what they eat, and how they are helpful. She organizes and displays this information on a web drawn on a piece of large paper, a transparency, or the board. She writes the topic *earthworms* in the large center circle. Spokes lead from the center circle to six smaller circles with the words *look*, *live*, *dig*, *move*, *eat*, and *help*. The teacher will add spokes from these smaller circles to the information students give her after reading the book.

A web is a wonderful way to organize information so that students can see what they are learning through reading. A web, like other graphic organizers, helps students become active readers when they search for more information about the topics displayed.

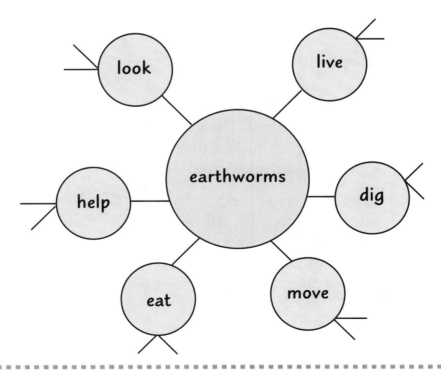

Comparison Charts

Another way to organize the information in *Wonderful Worms* is with a chart that has two columns. The first column is labeled *Worms*. The second column is labeled *Us*. The headings are *Where They Live, Body Parts, How They Dig*, and *What They Eat*. Students read to find out information about worms and add information about themselves from prior knowledge.

	<u>Worms</u>	<u>Us</u>
Where They Live		
Body Parts		
How They Dig		
What They Eat		

Story Maps

Story maps are graphic organizers that help students organize information from stories they read. Story maps help students think about important story elements, including setting, characters, and plot. The story-mapping format begins with the name of the book and the author. Then, the setting (when, where), characters (who), the problem/story events (beginning, middle, end), and conclusion are all added to the map.

Before reading, the teacher and students talk about each box on the story map. The teacher tells students that they will fill in the map together after reading. Students who finish reading before the group comes back together should take notes on things that they think belong in the different boxes on the map. There are many different kinds of story maps. One possible format is shown on page 73.

My Story Map

Name of story/book _____
Author _____

| Setting: | When | Where |

| Characters: | Who |

Problem:
    Beginning
    Middle
    End

Conclusion:

The Beach Ball

The beach ball is not a story map, but it can lead to the development of written story maps. The teacher uses a large beach ball with a question written in black permanent marker on each stripe of the ball:

- What is the book title, and who is the author?

- Who are the main characters?

- What is the setting?

- What happens in the story?

- How does the story end?

- What is your favorite part?

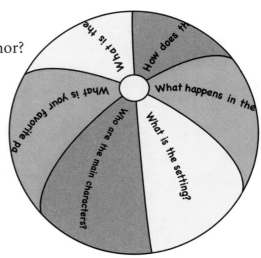

After reading a story, the teacher and students form a large circle. The teacher begins by tossing the ball to a student. The first student to catch the ball may answer any question on the ball. That student then tosses the ball to another student. This student may add to the answer given by the first student or answer another question. Students continue to throw the ball until all of the questions have been thoroughly answered. Some questions, such as those asking students to tell what happens in the story and to share their favorite parts, will have many different answers.

The beach ball is a favorite activity in all classrooms, including those with intermediate-aged students. In classrooms in which the teacher regularly uses the beach ball to follow up story reading, students begin to anticipate, as they read, the answers they will give to the questions on the stripes. These students have developed a clear sense of story structure, and their comprehension (and memory!) increases as they organize what they read by thinking about the questions written on the beach ball's stripes.

"Doing" the Book

Kids love to do things, and that includes reading. A popular follow-up to reading is the reenactment of the selection, with various students playing different parts as the rest of the class reads or tells the story.

Here is an example for *Three Cheers for Tacky* by Helen Lester. The first reading of this book was described in the Everyone Read To . . . (ERT) section (see pages 63–65). Now, it is time for the second reading. All students will get to act out the penguins' roles since the actors will change every five or six pages.

The teacher has made penguin pictures on which the penguins' names are written: Goodly, Lovely, Angel, Neatly, Perfect, and Tacky. She distributes these six name tags to six students and asks these students to come to the front of the classroom. The rest of the students and the teacher read the sentences together, stopping when actions are indicated for any or all of the penguins.

The class reads, "There once lived a group of penguins in a nice, icy land. One was Goodly." The student with the Goodly name tag steps forward, looking proud. "One was Lovely." The student playing Lovely steps forward, looking very proud.

One at a time, the penguins are introduced and step forward. When Tacky steps forward, he looks not proud but tacky. (The actors may need some direction from the teacher on how to look proud, tacky, etc.)

On the next pages, the teacher and students read about how the penguins go to school. Students act like they are reading books, writing their names, and learning numbers. Tacky, of course, reads, writes, and learns numbers quite differently from the other five penguins.

After five pages, the teacher and class applaud the actors. Then, the actors take their seats so that another group of students can become penguins. The new penguins put on the name tags and act out the next several pages in which the penguins practice cheers for the cheering contest. The teacher chooses a third set of penguins for the next several pages of cheering practice.

For the final pages of the book, all students are needed as actors. The teacher gives the Goodly, Lovely, Angel, Neatly, Perfect, and Tacky name tags to students who have not yet had them and then gives someone a judge name tag. There are three other teams in the competition, so the teacher divides the remaining students into these three teams. The teacher reads now, and one team of penguins does their cheer. The judge looks bored. The second team does their cheer, and the judge yawns. The third team does their cheer, and the judge snores. Finally, Tacky's team does their cheer. Tacky's odd antics wake up the judge, and his team captures the prize!

Building comprehension strategies is a major goal of Guided Reading. When students "do" the book, they think about all of the important story elements—characters, settings, actions, and sequence of events. The benefits of acting out the book as a regular Guided Reading format become obvious when students come to expect that they will act out the reading selection. If students know that they might act out the story, they think about who they would like to be from the story and what they would do if they were those characters. This kind of thinking greatly increases their comprehension.

"Doing" the book is especially helpful for students who are not fluent in English. Watching and being a part of the enactment helps build vocabulary and gives students a nonthreatening way to practice their reading and English skills.

Writing Connected to Reading

There are a variety of ways in which writing is used to increase comprehension:

- The paragraph frame (page 62) described as the culminating activity for Book Club groups is one way to increase comprehension.

- Sometimes, the writing is shared writing, for example, when selected students share something they have written in the Author's Chair.

- Students practice writing when they write down the ideas they want to add to a KWL chart or graphic organizer. These completed KWL charts and graphic organizers can also be used as frames for story summaries or informational paragraphs.

All students have opinions, and they love to tell you what they think. Writing prompts, which ask for their opinions, might include the following:

- My favorite part is . . .

- My favorite character is . . .

- I like (do not like) this book because . . .

- The funniest part is . . .

- The most interesting things I learned are . . .

Writing can also be used to help students think beyond the text. After reading *Three Cheers for Tacky* (pages 63–65 and 75–76), students might do one of the following activities:

- Write a different ending.

- Write about another person or animal they know who is different.

- Research and write about real penguins.

The Self-Selected Reading Block

GOALS

30-40 min.

- To share different kinds of literature through the teacher read-aloud
- To encourage students' reading interests
- To provide instructional-level reading materials
- To build students' intrinsic motivation for reading

Historically called individualized reading or personalized reading (Veatch, 1959), Self-Selected Reading time is now often labeled Reader's Workshop (Routman, 1995). Regardless of what it is called, **Self-Selected Reading is the part of a balanced literacy program during which students get to choose what they want to read and to which parts of their reading they want to respond. Opportunities are provided for students to share and respond to what is read. Teachers hold individual conferences with students about their books.**

The Self-Selected Reading Block includes the following:

- **The block begins with a teacher read-aloud.** The teacher begins the block by reading to students from a wide range of literature.

- **Students read on their own levels from a variety of books.** Books in the classroom library include books related to themes that the class is studying, easy and hard library books, old favorites, and easy, predictable books. Every effort is made to have the widest possible range of genres and levels available.

- **The teacher conferences with students.** While students read, the teacher conferences with several students each day.

- **Opportunities are provided for students to share what they are reading with each other.**

Self-Selected Reading

30-40 min.

Because all students are read to from a variety of books and they have time to read books that they have selected on their own, Self-Selected Reading probably varies less across classrooms, grade levels, and time of year than any other block. Still, there are some differences you would notice if you visited a Four-Blocks classroom during this block.

Teacher Read-Aloud

10 min.

Becoming a Nation of Readers (Anderson, Hiebert, Scott, & Wilkinson, 1985) asserts that **reading aloud to students is the single most important activity for creating the motivation and background knowledge essential for success in reading. It is hard to imagine any other activity that is so simple to do yet has so many benefits, such as the following:**

- Building students' motivation for becoming lifelong readers

- Increasing students' background knowledge on many topics

- Developing students' listening and speaking vocabularies which is important for all students but is critical for students who are learning English as a second language

- Teaching students about story elements and structure—stories have characters, settings, and problems or goals that are resolved in some way

- Giving students ideas for writing from books they have heard and showing them how authors create many different kinds of books

- Providing vicarious experiences for students with limited firsthand experience—books can take them to a big city, to a desert, back in time to the days of the pioneers, and forward in time to colonies on the moon, and multicultural books can help students learn to appreciate different people and places

Variations in Read-Aloud Material

Variety—which is important in all teaching activities—is particularly important in the choice of books read aloud to students. When teachers are asked to list several books that they have read aloud in the past month, some of the most popular titles include *Swimmy* by Leo Lionni, *Make Way for Ducklings* by Robert McCloskey, *Strega Nona* by Tomie dePaola, *Ira Sleeps Over* by Bernard Waber, and *The Mouse and the Motorcycle* by Beverly Cleary. Seldom has a teacher mentioned an informational book about animals,

an informational book about sports, an informational book about another country, a biography, a mystery, or a book of poetry. Often, the only books that teachers report reading to students are fiction—stories and chapter books. A nationwide survey of 537 elementary classroom teachers (Hoffman, Roser, & Battle, 1993) found that **not one of the most frequently listed read-aloud titles at any grade level was a nonfiction book.**

This predominance of fiction over nonfiction for teacher read-aloud choices makes sense if you consider that, until very recently, most children's books were stories. **In the last decade, however, many of the best new children's books have been nonfiction titles.** Authors such as Gail Gibbons, Joanna Cole, and Seymour Simon have created collections of truly informing books.

Stories should be a part of every teacher's read-aloud program, but not all students like stories. Many students want to learn about real things. The world of children's books has expanded enormously in the past decade. There is something for everyone out there. We believe that **a student who does not like to read is a student who has not found the right book.** Reading aloud from a variety of books—easy books, challenging books, one-sitting books, chapter books, mysteries, biographies, rhyming books, and all kinds of informational books—will help all students realize that there are books out there that they can't wait to read.

Read-Aloud Books Recommended by Primary Teachers

Storybooks

Alexander and the Terrible, Horrible, No Good, Very Bad Day by Judith Viorst (Atheneum, 1972)

Amelia Bedelia books by Peggy Parish (Harper & Row)

Arthur books by Marc Brown (Little, Brown & Co.)

A Chair for My Mother by Vera B. Williams (HarperTrophy, 1984)

Chrysanthemum and other picture books by Kevin Henkes (HarperTrophy, 1996)

Click, Clack, Moo: Cows That Type by Doreen Cronin (Simon & Schuster, 2000)

My Rotten Redheaded Older Brother by Patricia Polacco (Simon & Schuster, 1994)

Oliver Button Is a Sissy by Tomie dePaola (Harcourt Brace, 1979)

The Snowy Day by Ezra Jack Keats (Puffin, 1976)

Suddenly! by Colin McNaughton (Harcourt Brace, 1998)

Beginning Chapter Books

Amber Brown books by Paula Danziger (Scholastic)

Henry and Mudge books by Cynthia Rylant (Aladdin Paperbacks)

Junie B. Jones books by Barbara Park (Knopf)

Magic Tree House series by Mary Pope Osborne (Random House)

Marvin Redpost series by Louis Sachar (Random House)

Chapter Books

Charlie and the Chocolate Factory by Roald Dahl (Knopf, 1973)

Charlotte's Web by E. B. White (Harper & Row, 1953)

James and the Giant Peach by Roald Dahl (Puffin, 1996)

Ramona Quimby, Age 8 by Beverly Cleary (Morrow, 1981)

Travelers through Time #1: Back to the Titanic! by Beatrice Gormley (Turtleback, 1994)

Scary/Mystery Books

Boxcar Children mysteries by Gertrude Chandler Warner (Scholastic)

Cam Jansen mysteries by David A. Adler (Puffin Books)

Encyclopedia Brown mysteries by Donald J. Sobol (Bantam Books)

Franklin and the Thunderstorm by Paulette Bourgeois (Scholastic, 1998)

Franklin in the Dark by Paulette Bourgeois (Scholastic, 1987)

Nate the Great series by Marjorie Weinman Sharmat (Cowan, McCann, Inc.)

There's a Nightmare in My Closet by Mercer Mayer (Dial, 1968)

There's an Alligator under My Bed by Mercer Mayer (Dial, 1987)

Biographies

Johnny Appleseed by Gini Holland (Raintree/Steck, 1997)

Grandma Moses by Alexandra Wallner (Holiday House, 2004)

A Picture Book of Abraham Lincoln by David A. Adler (Holiday House, 1990)

A Picture Book of George Washington by David A. Adler (Holiday House, 1989)

A Picture Book of Martin Luther King, Jr. by David A. Adler (Holiday House, 1989)

Other David A. Adler picture book biographies (Holiday House)

Alphabet Books

A Is for Africa by Jean Carey Bond (Franklin Watts, 1969)

A My Name Is Alice by Jane Bayer (Dial, 1984)

The Accidental Zucchini: An Unexpected Alphabet by Max Grover (Harcourt, 1993)

Alphabatics by Suse MacDonald (Bradbury Press, 1987)

Eating the Alphabet: Fruits and Vegetables from A to Z by Lois Ehlert (Harcourt Brace Jovanovich, 1989)

Dr. Seuss's ABC by Dr. Seuss (Random House, 1960)

Books of Poetry

A Light in the Attic by Shel Silverstein (Harper & Row, 1981)

Make a Joyful Sound: Poetry for Children by African-American Poets edited by Debby Slier (Checkerboard, 1991)

Miles of Smiles: Kids Pick the Funniest Poems Book # 3 by Bruce Lansky (Meadowbrook Press, 1988)

Miss Mary Mack and other Children's Street Rhymes by Joanna Cole and Stephanie Calmenson (Morrow Jr. Books, 1990)

The New Kid on the Block by Jack Prelutsky (Greenwillow Books, 1984)

Where the Sidewalk Ends by Shel Silverstein (Harper & Row, 1974)

Informational Books, Math

The Coin Counting Book by Rozanne Lanczak Williams (Charlesbridge, 2000)

Eating Fractions by Bruce McMillan (Scholastic, 1992)

The Hershey's™ Kisses Addition Book by Jerry Pallotta (Scholastic, 2001)

The Hershey's™ Milk Chocolate Bar Fractions Book by Jerry Pallotta (Scholastic, 1999)

Midnight Math: Twelve Terrific Math Games by Peter Ledwon (Holiday House, 2000)

Reese's™ Pieces: Count by Fives by Jerry Pallotta (Scholastic, 2000)

Informational Books, Science

Bugs! Bugs! Bugs! by Jennifer Dussling (DK Children, 1999)
Dinosaurs by Gail Gibbons (Holiday House, 1987)
Everybody Needs a Rock by Byrd Baylor (Scribner, 1974)
Growing Up Wild: Penguins by Sandra Markle (Atheneum, 2002)
The Magic School Bus series by Joanna Cole (Scholastic)

Informational Books, Social Studies

Back Home by Gloria Jean Pinkney (Dial, 1992)
Duck for President by Doreen Cronin (Simon & Schuster, 2004)
Happy 4th of July, Jenny Sweeney by Leslie Kimmelman (Albert Whitman, 2003)
. . . If You Sailed on the Mayflower in 1620 by Ann McGovern (Four Winds Press, 1966)
I Have a Dream by Margaret Davidson (Scholastic, 1986)
Ox-Cart Man by Donald Hall (Viking, 1979)
So You Want to Be President? by Judith St. George (Philomel Books, 2001)

Fiction Books that Build Concepts

Anno's Counting Book by Mitsumasa Anno (Crowell, 1977)
Chicken Soup with Rice by Maurice Sendak (Harper & Row, 1962)
The Crayon Counting Book by Pam Munoz Ryan and Jerry Pallotta (Charlesbridge, 1996)
Exactly the Opposite by Tana Hoban (Greenwillow, 1978)
The Jolly Postman or Other People's Letters by Janet and Allan Ahlberg (Little, Brown & Co., 1986)

Classics

Any fairy tales, folktales, or collections of tales
Charlotte's Web by E. B. White (Harper & Row, 1953)
Curious George by Margret and H. A. Rey (Houghton Mifflin, 1973)
Little Red Riding Hood by John S. Goodall (McElderry, 1988)
Make Way for Ducklings by Robert McCloskey (Viking, 1976)
Winnie-the-Pooh books by A. A. Milne (E. P. Dutton, 1954)

Favorite Authors

David A. Adler
Marc Brown
Doreen Cronin
Gail Gibbons
Kevin Henkes

Mary Pope Osborne
Peggy Parish
Barbara Park
Cynthia Rylant
Vera B. Williams

Independent Reading and Conferencing
Variations in Where Students Read

15-20 min.

Tables with Book Crates

Perhaps the most noticeable difference between Four-Blocks classrooms would be where students are during Self-Selected Reading. In some Four-Blocks classrooms, students are at their desks and they read from crates of books that rotate from table to table. Each crate contains a wide range of levels and types of books, and students choose books from the crates on their tables. Classrooms that use the crates usually have a reserved book system. A student who is in the middle of a book from a particular crate, which will be moving on, can reserve that book by putting a special reserved bookmark in it. Students love having favorite books on reserve for themselves!

Centers

In other Four-Blocks classrooms, you will see students reading at a variety of centers, such as the following:

- A big-book center
- A magazine center
- A class-authored book center
- A science center that includes informational books on the current science topic
- A center full of books by a particular author being studied
- A recorded book read-along center
- A computer center with a book on CD-ROM

At Self-Selected Reading time, students go to these centers. In some classrooms, they rotate through the centers on different days, and in other classrooms, they choose the center to which they want to go.

Book Crates and Centers Combined

In still other classrooms, the crate and the center variations are combined. On Monday, half of the students read from the rotating crates of books at their desks, while the other half read at centers. On Tuesday, this is reversed. This variation is particularly helpful in small classrooms, where there are not many spaces for centers and where students would be crowded together at their tables if they were all reading there. Young students tend to vocalize as they read. They are taught to use whisper voices, but it is still not a silent time! Everyone's concentration is improved when there is as much distance between students as possible.

Regardless of where students are, classrooms with successful Self-Selected Reading time rigorously enforce the "no wandering" rule: "Once you get to your spot, you stay there!" In fact, in many classrooms, when students wander from their centers or do not appear to be engaging in the books there, they are sent back to their desks. After a few times, students seldom need to be sent back.

Conference Variations

Once the Self-Selected Reading Block gets up and running and students know where to go and how to read during this time, teachers usually hold individual conferences with students. **This critical conference time is how this block differs from other models of silent sustained reading or DEAR** (Drop Everything And Read).

It is important for teachers to model that they are also readers, that they enjoy personal reading, and that reading is a vital part of their everyday lives. Teachers must find appropriate times, other than during conferences, to share what they enjoy reading, such as taking a moment during the circle time at the beginning of the day to say, "When I got home yesterday, I sat down to read the newspaper and came across this funny article about a mother duck and her ducklings strolling down the interstate. I brought it to share with you today." Students need to know that reading and writing are useful and enjoyable beyond the classroom. **The conference time, however, provides some of the only one-to-one, individual time afforded to students throughout the school day.**

There are a couple of ways to hold a conference. **Some teachers go to where students are reading and conference with them there. Other teachers sit at a table and call students over to conference with them.**

Basic Conference Procedure

First, most teachers ask each student to read a page or two from the chosen book to make sure that the student is reading on level.

The teacher may then ask a general question or two:

- Why did you choose this book?
- Have you read any other book(s) by this author? If yes, which one(s)?
- Is your book fiction or nonfiction? How can you tell?
- What do you think will happen next? Why do you say that?
- How does the author make the facts interesting in this book? Show me an example.

The teacher also encourages students to look at reading from a writer's point of view:

- How does the author let you know that the main character is scared?
- Why is the beach a good setting for the story?
- If you had written this story, would you have chosen the same setting? Why or why not?
- Did you learn anything from this book that you can use in your own writing? If yes, what?

If students have been working on a particular comprehension skill during Guided Reading, the teacher may ask questions that help the student apply these skills to the book he has chosen:

- Who are the characters?
- What is the setting?
- Is there a problem, and does it get solved?
- Can you tell me what happens at the beginning, in the middle, and at the end of your story?
- What new facts did you learn from this book?
- Tell me about the pictures in the book and what you learned from them.
- Can you explain this chart about the parts of the animal's body to me?
- Can you read the map and explain where she traveled?

All students like to tell what they think. **Use open-ended questions to help them form opinions and tell about their reading preferences:**

- Do you like this book? Why or why not?
- What do you like about this book?
- What don't you like about this book?
- What is your favorite part?
- Who is your favorite character? Why?
- Does the book have any pictures you really like? If yes, which one(s)?
- What is the most interesting thing that you learned in this book?
- What is the funniest (saddest, most surprising, silliest, strangest) part of this book?

As the year progresses and students become fluent readers, there is more discussion and less reading aloud during the conference time. With fluent readers, reading aloud is used mostly to support the discussion.

Variations in Conference Focus

Occasionally, the teacher may want to help students anticipate the focus of the conference. In a classroom in which a teacher has been stressing a certain skill or strategy during the Guided Reading or Writing Block, the teacher may say to students, "We've been studying how important the setting can be to a story. When you bring your book to share with me this week, let's talk about the setting of your book and whether it's important to the story."

The teacher may want to remind them, "If you're reading an informational book, you probably won't have a setting, because that's something writers include when telling a story."

Bookmarks

When students begin to read chapter books, teachers may want to give each student a few bookmarks. These are used to mark the places of story elements or interesting information found during reading that the student may wish to discuss during the conference time. This could help save time during the conference because the student won't have to thumb through pages looking for something. Also, in an unobtrusive way, the bookmarks could serve to remind the student about the elements of the story as he is reading.

A set of bookmarks can be duplicated in an array of colors for each student and kept in student reading folders or in the book baskets. Be sure to include some bookmarks that focus on enjoyment, such as a favorite part of the book, a really neat description, and an "I didn't know that!" discovery. Students should use only one or two bookmarks during a sitting, since placing the bookmark should not become the main focus of reading. Enjoyment should always be the focus!

Conference Scheduling and Focus

Some teachers assign students specific days and conference with each student on his day, spending three or four minutes with him. Each student knows that on his day, he should bring one book to share with the teacher. He reads a few pages to the teacher, discusses the book, and tells why he chose it.

Book Choices

The major purpose of the reading conference is to encourage, help, and support students' independent reading. How much reading aloud is done, the types of questions asked, and the support offered by the teacher depend on the needs of each student. While letting students choose their own books is critical, teachers sometimes suggest books and authors they think students would enjoy.

If students consistently pick books that are much too easy for them, teachers may recommend more challenging books:

- "I know you like books about animals. This animal book is a little bit harder, but it has a lot of information and you are a good reader. I think that you can handle it. Why not try this book and let me know in our conference next week if it was too hard or just right and whether you liked it."

- "I bet you would enjoy reading some chapter books like the chapter book I'm reading to the class now. Here are three chapter books that a lot of good readers your age like to read as their first chapter books. Do you think that you might like to read one of these?"

Likewise, if students select books that are much too hard, teachers may show them how to choose books closer to their levels:

- "The book you brought today is a good book, but it seems awfully hard. Here are some books that are like the book you chose and that I think you would enjoy more. Let's try a few pages in one of these books and see if you like it and can read it better."

- Some teachers teach students the "five finger rule." Each student places a finger on her desk for every word in the text she doesn't understand. If a student has five fingers or more on the desk by the end of the page, the book is probably too hard for her to read alone.

- Some students are reading chapter books at home and want to continue reading them at school and conference with the teacher about them. While a lot of books are available in the classroom, students should also be encouraged to bring appropriate books from home or the library.

Assessment

While most of the conference time is spent talking with students about books and encouraging their reading interests, this time is occasionally used to assess how well students are progressing. If a new student moves into your class, you might use the conference time with that student to determine his reading level. In some schools, teachers use the conference time just before report cards to take running records and get other information about how well students are progressing in reading.

Teachers in Four-Blocks classrooms usually have a folder for each student in which they record information they learn through the conference. Some prefer having a conference form with particular reading skills or strategies listed that they can check as having observed or not observed. Some teachers prefer to strictly make anecdotal notes, from which they can later characterize progress over several weeks. A teacher may note that "Briana is unable to identify any of the characters in her story," "Jonas stops at unknown words and does not draw on any strategies to decode," "Michael was able to read aloud four pages of print in his book today!" or "Xander used context clues twice to decode unknown words." Although the anecdotal records a teacher keeps are an important part of documenting progress, the teacher must work hard at not letting the student feel that information gathering is more important than the personal book chat that the two of them are having.

Sharing Variations

5-10 min.

It is also important that students get to share books with each other. The sharing time usually brings closure to the Self-Selected Reading Block each day.

In most classrooms, the Self-Selected Reading Block ends with a Reader's Chair in which one or two students each day get to do a book talk. They show a favorite book, read or tell a little about the book, and try to "sell" this book to the rest of the class.

Their selling techniques appear to be quite effective, since these books are usually quickly seen in the hands of many of their classmates. Like adults, students like to be reading the same books that their friends are reading.

Some teachers have creative ways to encourage even the shyest of students to share with the whole class:

- **Teachers designate a special "share chair" or "reader's chair" for students to use.**

- **Students seem to love speaking into a microphone to talk about their books.** Inexpensive microphones, even those from dollar stores that don't really amplify voices, seem to "bring out the ham" in students and help them project their voices so that everyone can hear them.

- **One clever teacher always has her sharing time in a corner of the classroom, where a cardboard replica of a large TV screen is hanging from the ceiling.** Students share books or make reports from behind the screen. Everyone loves being a TV star!

- **Other teachers have reading parties one afternoon every two or three weeks.** Students' names are pulled from a jar, and they form groups of three or four in which everyone gets to share his favorite book. Reading parties, like other parties, often include refreshments, such as popcorn or cookies. Students develop all kinds of tasty associations with books and sharing!

- **Still other teachers arrange occasional outings to allow their students to read to younger students in the school.** Each student selects a favorite book and reads it to a younger reading buddy. Especially for the weaker readers, the teacher allows appropriate time and support for practicing the books before sharing with others so that students become confident readers.

The Writing Block

GOALS

30-40 min.

- To have students view writing as a way of telling about things
- To develop fluent writing for all students
- To teach students to use correct grammar and mechanics in their writing
- To teach particular writing forms
- To allow students to learn to read through writing
- To maintain the motivation self-confidence and of struggling writers

One way students learn to read is by writing. For struggling readers, their own writing is sometimes the first thing they can read. The daily Writing Block is carried out in Writers' Workshop fashion (Graves, 1994; Routman, 1995; Calkins, 1998). **Here are the components of the Writing Block:**

5-10 min.

Mini-Lesson—Teacher Writing

The Writing Block begins with a 5- to 10-minute mini-lesson. The teacher works with the overhead or with a large piece of chart paper. He writes and models all of the things that writers do—although not all on one day! The teacher thinks aloud, decides what to write, and then writes. While writing, the teacher models looking at the Word Wall for a troublesome word and invents the spelling of a few big words.

20 min.

Student Writing and Teacher Conferencing

Next, students work on their own writing. Since students vary in their writing development and in the time they need for different tasks, they are at different stages of the writing process—starting a new piece, finishing a piece, revising, editing, and illustrating. While students write, the teacher conferences with individuals, helping them get pieces ready to publish. In most classrooms, teachers let students publish pieces when they have completed three to five good first drafts. The student chooses the best draft to publish and conferences with the teacher. At this point, spelling and mechanics are corrected so that everyone can read the published piece.

5-10 min.

Sharing (Author's Chair)

Each day, this block ends with the Author's Chair, in which several students share their works, whether they are a first draft or published pieces. It is a time when students can listen to what other students are writing. What students read in the Author's Chair gives others new ideas for their own writing.

Variations within the Writing Block

Depending on the time of year, you will see many variations in the Writing Block. Here are a few examples:

The Half-and-Half Format

At the beginning of the year, many second-grade teachers use half-and-half paper, which has drawing space on the upper half and a few writing lines on the bottom half. (This paper is also called story paper, and is sometimes described as half-ruled, which is why this is called the half-and-half format.)

Procedure

In second grade, teachers often use half-and-half paper at the beginning of the year. Begin your mini-lesson by putting a piece of half-and-half paper on the board (or a half-and-half-transparency on the overhead). You may say something like the following:

"In second grade, we often use paper on which you can write your sentences on the lines at the bottom and draw your picture at the top. If you want to draw your picture first, that is also fine."

(Some students find more to say when they look at the pictures they have drawn. However, be careful that students spend more time writing than drawing!)

Then, model this procedure. Write several sentences on the lines at the bottom, modeling how to look at the Word Wall for words that you know are there and how to stretch out other words. Then, draw a picture that goes with the writing.

Next, students do their writing. Some students may draw first but should write a sentence or two on their lines. Others may write two or three sentences then draw. Some will write several sentences. One or two students may fill up the lines and want to write on the backs of their papers. Go around and encourage students. If you are asked to spell a word, don't spell it, but rather, help the student stretch out the word and write at least some letters.

After 10 to 15 minutes, gather students in a circle to share their creations. You should respond positively to what they tell, including those few students who have only pictures. In a few weeks, with the help of the Word Wall, other words around the room, and a few coaching sessions to help them stretch out words, even the struggling students will write a sentence or two to go with their pictures.

Writing, Revising, Editing, and Publishing

The next move is to have students write on their own without teacher encouragement. The teacher can now spend the time when students are writing to help them revise, edit, and publish pieces. This is also the time when he begins to use the Author's Chair procedure in which each student on his Monday list shares on Monday one piece she has written since the previous Monday, the Tuesday students share one piece on Tuesday, and so on.

Once most students are writing, many teachers let them choose the type of paper they would like to use. Some teachers help students think about which type of paper will help them tell their story best: plain, half-and-half, formal handwriting paper ruled with the appropriate grade-level lines, or notebook paper. Some classes use lined notebooks for all of their writing. These teachers have students—those who can write on the lines—use every other line so that there is plenty of room left to edit. Of course, many young students cannot write on the lines, but they still enjoy writing in their notebooks.

When a class is writing, revising, editing, and publishing, there are some additional variations:

- **In most classrooms, teachers let a student publish a piece when she has completed three to five good first drafts.** (Of course, *good* is a relative term that varies from student to student!) When a student has the required number of first drafts, she chooses one to publish. The student may choose a friend to help with the revising and editing, or she may do some self-editing. Once the editing is done, the student signs up for a conference with the teacher, who helps the writer get the piece into publishable form. At this point, all spelling is fixed and the piece is tidied up mechanically, because a published piece should be something that everyone can read easily and of which the student is proud.

- While many teachers find the above procedure quite workable, **other teachers prefer to work with a third of their class each week.** These teachers divide the class into thirds, including one of their most capable and least able writers in each third. In week one, students in the first third edit and publish a piece while the other two-thirds of the class work on as many first drafts as they can. In week two, when the first third of the students have each published a piece, they go back to first-draft writing while the teacher works with the second third. In week three, the final third—who have been producing first drafts for two weeks and may have a lot from which to choose—get to publish a piece. Week 4 begins the cycle again.

- **There are variations in the publication form too,** including individual books; pieces copied, illustrated, and displayed on a class author board; class books; pieces typed and illustrated using a computer publishing program; and even some class-created Web pages.

Regardless of how the writing, revising, editing, and publishing process is structured, it is important that students spend more of their writing time doing the difficult (but important!) work of first-draft writing. It is during this time that students do much of the mental work—applying everything that they are learning during the other three blocks—that moves them along in reading and writing.

- As students use the Word Wall and other room resources to spell words and stretch out the spelling of longer words, **they are applying their word and phonics strategies.**

- **Students also apply their comprehension strategies** as they learn to keep their writing on topic, to put things in the right sequence, and to decide whether what they write is going to be real or make-believe.

- In the beginning, most students do not write stories. Their writing is more descriptive and personal. Once they learn more about stories from their reading, they like to try to write them. As they write stories, **students learn that each story must have a beginning, a middle, and an end. Students also begin to think about story elements, such as characters and setting.**

- **Students also write informational pieces, and they use what they are reading both to get information and as models for how to write information.**

A Variety of Mini-Lessons

Mini-lessons begin in a huddle in the front of the classroom. Students are close and can see you write as you talk about what you are doing and why. Some teachers let students sit in their seats to watch and listen. (If you are not getting quiet listeners, pull them in closer. It helps!) **Some mini-lessons are musts for all primary classrooms:**

- Choosing a Topic

- What to Do When You Can't Spell a Word

- Punctuation and Grammar

- Adding to a Piece

- Revising

- Editing

Margaret Defee, the pilot teacher for Four Blocks, taught us a lot of what we now know about the Author's Chair. She kept a list of the mini-lessons she taught. Mrs. Defee also kept a list of the books that her students published during the first year. There were more than 200 titles on that list, including the following:

I Built a Snowman	School	Toronto
My Friends	When I Moved	Space
The Lost Shoe	My Joke Book	Trick-or-Treating
Our Costumes	Easter	Grandma and Me
German Shepherds	Boxing	Paul Bunyan
Winter	My Race Car	Basketball
Bikes	Rocks	Lightning

Mini-lessons vary according to the time of year and the observed needs of students. Following are several sample mini-lessons that are essential at the beginning of the year, regardless of grade level and how well students write.

Great Ideas for Mini-Lessons*

1. Actual class procedures used during the writing period
2. Rules for the writing period made by the teacher and/or students
3. Teacher-modeled writing using think-alouds
4. Shared writing
5. "Words Authors Use" (Have a word a day. Examples: *publish, illustrate, edit, topic, dedicate,* etc.)
6. Grammar and Usage
   nouns—words that are people, places, things, or ideas
   verbs—words that show action
   adjectives—words that describe nouns
7. Uppercase letters
8. Punctuation marks
9. How to "set a scene" (create a setting)
10. Fiction
11. Nonfiction
12. Mysteries
13. Stories that teach
14. Feelings in writing
15. Read a book, any book! Books are great writing models.
16. How to add to or change a story
17. Staying on topic
18. Rhyming words
19. Synonyms
20. Homonyms
21. Antonyms
22. Poetry (This could turn into a week of mini-lessons.)
23. Letter writing
24. Interviews
25. Riddles
26. Jokes
27. Newspapers
28. How to make a list
29. Student pieces (Always use a piece that a student wrote correctly!)

*A successful mini-lesson is short, teacher-directed, and discusses only one topic.

Choosing a Topic

Procedure

The teacher begins this mini-lesson by telling students, "When you write, you should usually choose topics about which you know a lot."

Then, the teacher models how she chooses a topic to write about each day:

"Today, I could write about my favorite basketball team, Wake Forest University. They are playing the University of North Carolina tonight. When these two teams play each other, it is always a good basketball game . . . I could write about my daughter's new car. She is so excited about her first new car! I could also write about my cat, Tommy. He's such a rascal. I told you before that I had a cat named Tommy, but I didn't tell you very much about him. I think that I will write about my cat, Tommy."

The teacher then begins writing on a transparency or a large piece of chart paper so that all students can see. She talks as she writes:

"I can put the title, My Cat, here at the top because I know that I will write all about my cat. I begin the first sentence with a capital letter: 'My cat's name is Tommy.' I begin **Tommy** with a capital letter because names begin with capital letters.

He is fat and furry, so I will write that for my second sentence. Once again, I will begin with a capital letter for the first word in the sentence. I can spell **fat,** but I am not sure how to spell **furry.** Let me stretch out the word **furry** and listen for the letters that make those sounds: '**f-ur-re.**' When I am writing a new word and I am not sure that I spelled it correctly, I write it the best I can and I circle it. Circling a word means that I will check that word if I decide to publish this story later."

The teacher continues to talk about her cat and writes what she is saying:

"He likes everyone. He thinks that everyone likes him. Tommy is a rascal." (Stretching it out, she spells the last word **raskl.**)

After having written her five sentences, the teacher asks students to tell her things about which they know a lot. Hands go up, and the list begins. Students tell her about their pets, their families, their friends, and other topics in which they are interested. She concludes by saying, "Those all sound like good story topics to me! So, let's tiptoe back to our seats and begin to write about them."

Topic Chart

Some teachers keep charts in their classrooms on which, throughout the day, they write down topics about which they and students might like to write. For example, when a student comes in wearing new glasses, the teacher comments on them and adds *glasses* to the chart.

Topics We Might Write About

Glasses	Magnets
No Electricity	A New Student
Birthday Parties	Changing Schools
Going Camping	A New House
Penguins	A New Bike
How People Lived Long Ago	Motorcycles
A New Baby	Playing Basketball
Mr. Duncan, the Substitute Teacher	The Hundred Days Celebration
Miss Black, Our Student Teacher	

What to Do When You Can't Spell a Word

When elementary school students write, they cannot spell all of the words they want to use unless they limit what they say to words they can spell. Students can and will choose easy words if the teacher (or a parent) talks too much about spelling it correctly. When students limit their word choices, they no longer write about an enormous dinosaur, but they write about a big one. Food is not delicious; it is good. Friends are not fantastic or wonderful to play with; they are nice. **Students, whether eager or reluctant writers, need to feel free to express themselves and use the words they want to tell their stories.**

The Word Wall and other visible words in the room will help students with a lot of words, but there are many words young students have in their speaking vocabularies that are not in their reading or writing vocabularies. For these words, ask students to do what authors (and adults) do: say each word slowly, listen for the sounds they hear, and write the letters that those sounds represent. Sometimes, adults are right, and sometimes they are wrong—just like children! So, they circle each word and check its spelling later.

It is a good idea to have a What to Do When You Can't Spell a Word mini-lesson early in the school year. After that, model what you do about spelling for several words—but not all of the words—in each mini-lesson.

For this example mini-lesson, the teacher takes a big piece of chart paper or a transparency and begins to talk and write:

"Today, I will write about the snow we had yesterday. I'm beginning with a capital letter because sentences begin that way: Yesterday was January 28. I can find the words **January** and **yesterday** on our calendar board. **January** is at the top; it is the name of this month. I know that under the calendar, it says, 'Today is _____. Yesterday was _____. Tomorrow will be _____.' So, I can look there to find the word **yesterday**.

Once again, for the second sentence, I start with a capital letter. I write 'We **had six inches of snow**. (**Had** is easy because I can look on the Word Wall for it.) **six** (The word **six** is one of the number words in the front of our classroom.) **inches** (I look around the room for the word **inches**, and I don't see it. If it's not on the Word Wall and I cannot find it anywhere in the room, I'll stretch it out i-n-c-h-e-s.) of **snow** (I can find **snow** on the theme board, where all of the winter words are listed under winter pictures)."

The teacher follows the same thinking process when she writes her next three sentences:

"I made snowballs. I made a snowman. I had fun in the snow."

It is important to show students what good writers do when they need words they can't spell. **Authors don't stop writing to look up words. They keep writing, spell the words the best they can, and check them later.** Young students need to learn to have a spelling consciousness—that means spelling words as best as they can in the first draft and correcting them in the final draft. **Looking up words in the dictionary belongs in the editing stage, not in the first-draft stage.**

Adding On to a Piece

How can teachers get students to continue stories the next day? Continue a story in your mini-lesson, modeling the thought processes involved. For example, the teacher who wrote about the cat named Tommy (see page 99) continues her story the second day. She tells students that she did not write everything she knew about her cat and that there are a lot more things she could tell. She could tell where he likes to sleep and what he likes to eat. She could tell some stories about times when Tommy thought that he was a person and acted just like one.

Then, she takes out her piece from the day before, rereads what she has already written, and adds on to the story by starting a second paragraph:

> My cat thinks that he is a person. He likes to sleep on the bed. He puts his head on the pillow, just like I do! He likes to eat spaghetti. Sometimes, he eats popcorn when it falls on the floor.

The teacher can continue the piece for a third day if she thinks that her class is ready for more (maybe about a time when Tommy surprised everyone and made them laugh). When writing longer pieces, the teacher can edit each paragraph daily during the mini-lesson or spend the fourth day revising and editing all three. **There is no right or wrong time frame for this mini-lesson. Look at your students' writing to see what they need.**

My Cat

My cat's name is Tommy. He is fat and (furre.) He likes everyone. He thinks that everyone likes him. Tommy is a (raskl.)

First Day

My Cat

My cat's name is Tommy. He is fat and (furre.) He likes everyone. He thinks that everyone likes him. Tommy is a (raskl.)

My cat thinks that he is a person. He likes to sleep on the bed. He puts his head on the pillow, just like I do! He likes to eat spaghetti. Sometimes, he eats popcorn when it falls on the floor.

Second Day

Editing Checklist: Capitalization and Punctuation

Many states or school systems have a list of required language skills, which usually include capitalization, punctuation, and grammar. For years, these language skills were taught with worksheets and workbooks, but there was little transfer to students' writing. **Now, we know that for language skills to transfer to writing, they must be taught during writing.** Some mini-lessons should focus on the language skills of capitalization, punctuation, and grammar.

For capitalization, punctuation, and grammar, develop and gradually add to an Editing Checklist like the one below.

1. Name and date
2. Sentences make sense

3. Ending. ?!
4. Beginning capitals

5. Capitals for names

6. Possible misspellings circled
7. Title in center
8. Stays on topic

Note that items are added gradually. The first thing this teacher put on the checklist was "Name and date." This was the only thing on the checklist. Each day, as the teacher finished whatever writing he was doing for his mini-lesson, he pointed to the checklist and asked students to help him check to see whether he had included his name and the date. Some days, he had put both. Some days, he had put his name but not the date or the date but not his name. On other days, he had put neither. Students soon got into the habit of checking his writing for this and loved pointing out to him when he had "forgotten"!

Once the teacher began the checklist, he also began asking students to check their papers each day before putting them away. In a week's time, almost all students were automatically putting their names and the date on their papers every day. Those who forgot one or the other quickly added it when the writing time was up, and the teacher prompted them to check for it.

When almost all students have learned automatically to do one important, mechanical thing, it is time to add a second item. The teacher in the example added "Sentences make sense," and from that day on, students helped him check his writing for two things: Had he remembered to put his name and the date, and did all of the sentences make sense? During this time, he would usually write one sentence that did not make sense, either by leaving out a word, putting in a wrong word, or failing to finish the sentence. After checking for the name and date, the teacher and students would read each sentence together and decide whether it made sense and, if not, how to fix it.

Once there were two things on the list, the teacher asked students to read their own writing each day to make sure that they had included their names and dates and that all of the sentences made sense. Sometimes, it takes about a month for students to get into the habit of checking for these two things in their own writing. When the teacher notices that most students do this, it is time to add another item to the checklist. Students don't always find the sentences that don't make sense ("It made sense to me!"), but they know that writers reread their pieces to check for this.

Take signals from students for adding to the checklist. Don't expect them to become perfect at executing each item on the list but watch for them to know what they should be checking. **As the checklist and what students write each day get longer, students can't check for everything every day. Rather, they use the Editing Checklist to check their own first-draft writing before conferencing with the teacher.**

Parts of Speech

In addition to using the Editing Checklist, which is a part of almost every mini-lesson, **some mini-lessons should focus on the parts of speech—nouns, verbs, and adjectives—and their functions, which are a part of most primary language curriculums.** Most teachers begin to do some grammar mini-lessons during second grade. Again, take cues from students. When students are writing fluently, it is time to help them begin to look for better ways to say things.

One teacher who did this quite well wrote a story one day and read it to her class.

- The class then talked about nouns being words for people, places, things, and ideas. They looked for nouns in each sentence. Then, the teacher asked, "Could I have used a better word for **dog**? Could I have said that it was a **dalmatian** or a **dachshund**? When I wrote 'The dog ran down the street,' could I have used a better noun for **street**? Was it a **highway**, a **neighborhood street,** or a **country road**?"

- After looking for the nouns and replacing them with more-specific, more-descriptive words and phrases, the teacher talked about verbs, or action words. She then asked, "When I wrote 'The dog ran down the street,' should I have said 'The dog scampered' or 'The dog dashed'?"

- **The teacher helped students see that using more-specific nouns and verbs helps readers see their stories better.** She reminded them, "When you write today, or if you are revising, remember to look at the nouns and verbs and see if you can make your story even better!"

Many of her students were soon looking at their own pieces and adding better nouns and verbs.

One student in particular put into practice many of the skills from these mini-lessons. He first wrote an informational piece about bichon puppies. Then, he wrote a story about a bichon puppy, titled "A Long Ride Home." It is always rewarding when teachers can see firsthand that students are becoming better at writing!

Bichons by Brandon

A Bichon is a kind of dog. You can't be allergic to them, they do not shed and they are good with children. A Bichon puppy is about three inches long. You need to put a collar on them when they are 6 weeks old.

When they are puppies you will need to get them a chew toy because they will want to chew. A full-grown Bichon is about 1 foot tall and 24 inches long. They are really cute. When they are about 2 years old they will probably act like a kid. When they are puppies they will want to use paper. When they are older they will go outside to the bathroom.

A Long Ride Home by Brandon

One cold December day a Bichon mom named Bunny was having babies. They were born on December 10th. The runt of the group was named Frisco. He was the last one out of the mom. He was the first to get out of the box and the first one to go use the paper.

One January day a nice family of five came to bring him home. The boy's name was Weavil. The Weavils went in the house, got the puppy, went out, and got in the car. They soon left.

First the family stopped by a restaurant and got some food. They got home in two hours. Frisco was very excited, so he ran around. He was very happy to be at his new home. THE END

Revising and Editing

Many teachers write and edit during their mini-lessons every day, especially when the pieces they model are as short as the pieces that students write. As students' pieces get longer, so do the teacher's pieces. That makes writing and editing in 10 minutes more difficult. **Eventually, you may need to spend several days on a piece with your students: writing, adding on, and making it better by revising and editing.**

Other teachers show the class several good pieces written by students in the class and edit one piece to show how it is done. There is one rule for this: **It should not be an example of the best or the worst writing.** In one second-grade class, a boy wrote a piece about dinosaurs. He was such a good writer that it needed almost no revising and editing. A piece such as this is not a good piece to choose to model revising and editing, but it is a delight to the teacher and students.

Velociraptor

2 Velociraptor were hunting. They had seen a triceratops. A raptor pounced and became locked in combat too fierce for the other to enter. After a long battle neither of the two animals had won, both had killed the other in battle leaving the other raptor on his own. After scavenging some meat, he left in search of a new herd. A few days later the raptor had spotted a protoceratops nest. The eggs make an easy meal if it wasn't for one problem, an oviraptor. The slightly smaller predator was also eating the eggs, so the raptor would have to fight for a meal. The raptor moved toward the nest, then, slashing out with it's sickle-claws the velociraptor pounced scaring away the enemy and an easy fast-food stand. As the raptor feasted it heard a roar. Suddenly a Turbasaurus burst into view. The raptor saw another herd chasing Turbasaurus. The raptor decided to join the hunt. With his help, the herd brought down prey. He had found a pack.

Don't choose a piece that is hard to read or understand. **Choose something that is good but needs some work in order to be published.** This way, students can enjoy reading the piece and learn how to edit (peer-edit or self-edit) at the same time. Below is a story that a teacher used early in second grade to demonstrate this.

1. First, the teacher made a copy of the piece. Then, she made a transparency from the copy.

2. Using the transparency on the overhead, she let students read the original and tell the author what they liked about it.

3. Next, she asked for any suggestions that students might have for ways to make it better. Students made suggestions for more-specific words and a few sentences to add. The writer decided which suggestions to use in revising.

4. Finally, students made editing suggestions, such as fixing spelling, rewriting run-on sentences, and correcting some punctuation.

Rough Draft

My Cat Filex by Sarah

My cat's name is Filex. He same times palys arouad the house. He is funny. He sads on his bach feet when I hold chees in the air. And one time he juped up on the calner to get some cik-noodl soop. He likes me and my family. He like chees too. He is lasy sometimes.

Final Draft

My Cat Felix
by Sarah

My cat's name is Felix. He sometimes plays around the house. He is funny. He sits on his back feet when I hold cheese in the air. One time Felix jumped on the counter to get some chicken noodle soup. He likes my family. Felix likes cheese too. Sometimes, he is lazy. But I still like my cat Felix!

109

Focused Writing

Most of the writing done during the Writing Block in second grade follows the format just described. Teachers model a variety of topics and forms (genres) during the mini-lessons, but students choose their own topics and decide which forms to use.

Sometimes, however, the teacher wants all students to write about a specific topic or learn to write in a specific form. Alert students ahead of time that next week during writing time, they will be working on some writing as a class but that when the week is over, they will be able to get back to their own topics. Following are two examples of focused writing weeks.

Letters—Focused Writing

The teacher of this class has a good friend who is a teacher in another state. The two teachers decide that their students would enjoy being pen pals and exchanging letters. Students are excited about the idea—this is their first letter-writing experience. The teacher wants them to learn the correct form for a letter, while at the same time making sure that the emphasis is kept on the message.

 Brainstorming

The lesson begins with the teacher asking students what kinds of things they would like to know about their pen pals. He records these questions on a large sheet of paper.

It is clear that students have many things that they would like to know about their new pen pals. The teacher helps them organize their questions by beginning a web like the one on the next page.

Students help decide where the questions should go on the web. Then, they come up

Questions about Pen Pals
- How old are they?
- What is school like there?
- Do they have a gym?
- Do they have a lot of homework?
- Do they have a basketball team?
- Do they play basketball?
- Do they play baseball? Football? Soccer? Other sports?
- What is the weather like?
- What do they do with their friends?
- What do they like to eat?
- Do they have computers?
- Do they play video games?

with more questions, which are also written in the correct places on the web.

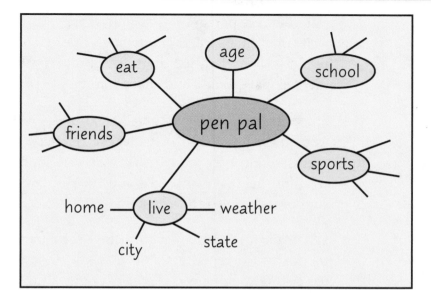

On the following day, the teacher and students review the web. The teacher points out that if these are some of the things that they would like to know about their pen pals, they are probably also some of the things that their pen pals are wondering about them. He explains that they can't possibly include all of this information in the first letter. He tells them that they will be writing back and forth all year and that as the year goes on, they will share and learn these and many other types of things.

 ## First Draft

The teacher goes to the overhead and leads students through the process of writing the first letter. He explains that because these letters will be read by their pen pals, each letter must be correct and readable. Today's task is to start a good first draft, which will be edited and recopied or typed later.

The teacher explains and models for students how and where to put the inside address, the date, and the greeting. Students watch as he does each step on the transparency. Then, they do the same steps on their papers.

Next, the teacher asks students to look at the web and decide what to write about in the first paragraph. The class decides that they should write about their personal facts. The teacher agrees and has them watch as he writes a paragraph that gives some personal facts about him.

After writing this first paragraph, the teacher reads it aloud, changing one word and adding another word to model how a writer reads and changes things as he writes. He points out the paragraph indentation and shows the class that his paragraph has four sentences. Then, he instructs students to write their first paragraphs, telling some personal facts about themselves. He reminds them that first drafts are always written on every other line so that there is space to add and change things later.

Students begin to write their paragraphs. As they write, they glance at the web on the board and at the teacher's letter on the overhead. It is clear that even though these students are not very sophisticated writers, the demonstration they have observed and the displayed web and letter provide the support they need to write a first draft.

When most students have finished their paragraphs, the teacher reminds them that good writers stop occasionally and read what they have written before moving on. He waits another minute while each student reads what she has written. He is encouraged when he sees students making a few changes based on their rereading.

The process of the teacher writing a paragraph, reading it aloud, making a few changes, and giving students time to write their own paragraphs continues that day and the next. The teacher and students construct paragraphs with information from the categories on the web. After each paragraph, students are reminded to reread and make any needed changes and additions. The teacher notices that when they get to later paragraphs, many students are automatically rereading and revising without being reminded to do so.

Finally, the teacher suggests possible closings and shows students where to put the closing. As they watch, he writes a closing on his letter, and they write theirs. This completes the first draft of the letters.

 ### Revising
On the next day, the teacher helps students polish their letters. He puts students into sharing groups of four and has each student read her letter. Just as with the Author's Chair, this sharing is focused on the message only. Listeners tell the author something they like, and the author asks them if anything is not clear or if they have suggestions for making the letter better.

When everyone in the group has had a chance to share, students make whatever revisions they choose. Students can be seen crossing out things and inserting additional information. As they do this, it becomes apparent why it is critical to write the first draft on every other line.

Editing

Now that the letters are revised and students are satisfied with their messages, it is time to do a final edit. Students are accustomed to choosing friends to help them edit drafts that they will publish, so they tailor this process to letters.

Students refer to the Editing Checklist displayed in the classroom and decide that the things for which they usually edit are still valid but that they need to change number 1 to correspond with letter editing. Number 1 had been "Name and date." They decide that for letters, number 1 should be "Address, date, greeting, and closing." Students then pair with friends and read for each thing on the checklist together. When they have finished helping each other edit, they share their drafts with the teacher during their final editing conferences.

Final Copy

On the following day, students choose some stationery and copy the letters in their most legible handwriting. Finally, the teacher demonstrates how to put the recipient's address and the return address on an envelope. (Even though he intends to mail all of the letters to the pen pals' school in one large envelope, he wants students to learn how to address envelopes. He also knows that individually sealed envelopes will help the pen pals feel like they are getting "real" letters.) The letters are mailed, and their writers eagerly await their replies. Next week, in a faraway city, this process begins again as the teacher's friend takes her class through the same steps of learning to write personal letters.

The procedure just described is not difficult, but it does take time. Most classes would spend at least five 30- to 40-minute sessions going through the brainstorming, webbing, modeling, first-draft writing, revising, and editing. The first time anything is done is always the hardest—for the teacher and students. A month later, when students have received their letters and are ready to write again, the process will be much easier and will go much more quickly. After three or four letters, most students will know how to organize information and will write interesting and correctly formed letters with minimal help. By the end of the year, they will be expert letter writers and will have gained a lot of general writing skills in the process.

Dear Will,

I live in Clemmons, North Carolina. I have a new house. It is near the Yadkin River. The weather is getting warmer because it is spring. In the summer it is hot here!

I am seven years old. I am in second grade. My teacher's name is Mr. Spencer. He reads to us every day and he is nice. My friends at school are Mitchell, Seth, and Kendra. We play soccer after school together. We are in a league. In the summer we swim together at the pool.

Please write back and tell me about Chicago and your second grade class.

Your friend,
Aidyn

Reports—Focused Writing

Teachers often ask students to write reports. If the class is studying animals, famous African Americans, or celebrations around the world, students are asked to choose one topic about which to write. **Teachers need to model how to write a report, not just assign one.** Reports are another form of focused writing in second grade.

Imagine that a class is doing a science unit on animals. The teacher has read aloud many animal books, and there are animal books on different reading levels available during Self-Selected Reading. There are also encyclopedias and several computers in the classroom.

Brainstorming

The teacher tells the class that they will take a week off from their individual writing to make a class book about animals. Together, they brainstorm the different animals about which they could write.

horses	cats	dogs	pigs	turtles
squirrels	snakes	bears	giraffes	frogs
fish	whales	pandas	tigers	owls
birds	rhinoceroses	bees	ducks	goats
elephants	mice	cows	chickens	sheep
geese	lions	iguanas	camels	coyotes
monkeys	penguins	zebras	foxes	dolphins
wolves	chipmunks	beavers	kangaroos	bats

Narrowing the Topic

The teacher tells students that each one of them will become an expert on one type of animal and write about it. Because she knows that some animals will be more popular than others, she asks them to write down the names of five animals about which they would want to write. She then assigns each student an animal on which to become an expert. The teacher chooses an animal that no one else has chosen—the pig!

Finding Out Things

Together, the teacher and students come up with questions that her report on pigs should answer.

The teacher writes each question on one large index card, and she labels another card, "Other Interesting Facts."

What do they eat?	How long do they live?	Where do they live?
Are they smart?	Are pigs and hogs the same?	How big are they?
Are they really dirty?	What body parts do they have?	Do they hibernate?
Other Interesting Facts		

Next, the teacher gives students large index cards and asks them to think of questions about their animals. She helps them see that some of their questions (for example, *What do they eat? Where do they live?*) might be just like hers but that they should have questions (for example, *Are pigs and hogs the same thing?*) that are specific to their animals as well. She also tells them that there will be other interesting facts about their animals that they should put on their Other Interesting Facts cards. Students begin to write their questions, and the teacher helps them.

Reading, Researching, and Taking Notes

For the next several days, the teacher gathers students and together they do research on pigs. She puts the index cards in the pocket chart. She has written the questions as large as possible with a thick marker so that all students can see them. As she reads about pigs from books and encyclopedias, students stop her when they hear something that answers one of the questions or when they want to add a fact to the Other Interesting Facts card. She writes this information in smaller print on the cards. (It is important for students to be able to see the questions so that they know where information will go, but they don't need to see the notes about the questions.) Students and the teacher are amazed to learn that pigs are baby hogs and that they can really be called pigs only until they are 10 weeks old! The teacher reads and takes notes on pigs for about 15 minutes.

Then, students take their cards to places where they can spread them out and do research on their animals. The teacher moves around the room and helps students as they record facts on their cards.

Writing the Report

After several days of taking notes, the teacher and students are ready to begin writing their reports. The teacher models how she decides which information to include in each paragraph. Next, students begin their reports, and the teacher helps them decide how to organize their notes. When all of the first drafts are written, students work with partners to revise and edit them. The teacher does a final edit, and the reports are typed on the computer, illustrated, and bound into a class book.

Just as for the focused writing lesson on letter writing, the first focused report-writing lesson takes a lot of time and effort. In a month or so, however, when the class works together to do biographies of famous Americans, the process goes much more quickly and the learning that took place during the first lesson becomes obvious. By participating in several focused report-writing lessons, all students learn how to write informational articles without copying from books.

The Working with Words Block

GOALS

- To teach students how to read and spell high-frequency words
- To teach students how to decode and spell other words using patterns from known words
- To have students automatically and fluently use phonics and spelling patterns while reading and writing

30 min.

In the Working with Words Block, students learn to read and spell high-frequency words and to recognize patterns that allow them to decode and spell many additional words. This chapter describes the activities that make up the Working with Words Block. Of course, these activities vary greatly depending on the grade level and the time of year.

Word Walls

Word Walls in Second Grade

10 min.

Many second-grade teachers start the Word Wall by putting students' names on it, adding five names each day rather than five names for the week. When doing names in second grade, they clap and cheer them. Then, they write them. Once the names are on the Word Wall, five words are added each week.

Second-grade teachers choose their Word Wall words each week from high-frequency (not vocabulary!) words in their reading selections and high-frequency words that students are misspelling in their writing. Many second-grade Word Wall words are repeats from first grade. That is because all second graders have not mastered the spelling of many important high-frequency four-letter words. They can read them now in second grade, but they still can't write them correctly! For example, second-grade Word Walls often repeat some first-grade words, such as **they**, **said**, **have**, **come**, **when**, **what**, **went**, **want**, and **your**.

Once the hard-to-spell, high-frequency words are on the wall, the teacher should try to include the following:

- An example word for each letter combination, including **ch, sh, th, wh, qu, ph, wr,** and **kn**

- Examples for the less common **c** and **g** sounds

- Words representing the most common blends: **bl, br, cl, cr, dr, fl, fr, gr, pl, pr, sk, sl, sm, sn, sp, st,** and **tr**

- Examples for the most common vowel patterns:

  a: **cr<u>a</u>sh, m<u>a</u>ke, r<u>ai</u>n, pl<u>ay</u>ed, c<u>ar</u>, s<u>aw</u>, c<u>augh</u>t**
  e: **w<u>e</u>nt, <u>ea</u>t, gr<u>ee</u>n, sist<u>er</u>, n<u>ew</u>**
  i: **<u>i</u>nto, r<u>i</u>de, r<u>igh</u>t, g<u>ir</u>l, th<u>i</u>ng**
  o: **n<u>o</u>t, th<u>o</u>se, fl<u>oa</u>t, <u>or</u>, <u>ou</u>tside, b<u>oy</u>, sh<u>oo</u>k, sch<u>oo</u>l, h<u>ow</u>, sl<u>ow</u>**
  u: **b<u>u</u>g, <u>u</u>se, h<u>ur</u>t**
  y: **wh<u>y</u>, ver<u>y</u>**

- The most commonly written contractions: **can't, didn't, don't, it's, that's, they're,** and **won't**

- Homophones: **to, too, two; there, their, they're; right, write; one, won;** and **new, knew**

- Example words with **s, ed,** and **ing** endings

Second-Grade Word Wall List

Below is a list of words that a Word Wall might contain at the end of second grade. Starred words have spelling patterns that help students spell a lot of rhyming words. A clue (shown in parentheses) is attached to some homophones so that students can tell which homophone is which. (A clue can be an opposite word, picture, etc.)

about	girl	our	then*
after	green	outside	there (here)
again	gym	people	they
are	have	phone*	they're
beautiful	here	played*	(they are)
because	house	pretty	thing*
before	how*	quit*	those
best*	hurt	rain*	to
black*	I	really	too (Too
boy*	into	ride*	late!)
brothers	it's	right*	trip*
bug*	joke*	(Wrong!)	truck*
can't	jump*	said	two (2)
car*	junk*	sale*	use
caught	kicked*	saw*	very
children	knew*	school*	wanted
city	line*	shook*	was
clock*	little	sister	went*
could	made*	skate*	were
crash*	mail*	slow*	what
crashes	make*	small*	when*
didn't	many	snap*	where
don't	more*	sometimes	who
drink*	name*	sports*	why*
eating*	new* (old)	stop*	will*
every	nice*	tell*	with
favorite	not*	than*	won
first	off	thank*	won't
float*	one (1)	that's	write*
found*	or	their	writing
friends	other	them	

Doing a Word Wall

The first 10 minutes of this block are spent "doing" the Word Wall words. *Doing* a Word Wall is not the same as *having* a Word Wall. *Having* a Word Wall might mean putting up all of these words somewhere in the room and telling students to use them. In many cases, struggling readers can't use the words, because they don't know them!

Teachers who *do* Word Walls (rather than just *have* Word Walls) report that *all* of their students can learn these critical words. Here is the procedure:

Each week, select five words and add them to a wall or bulletin board in the room. The Word Wall grows as the year progresses. Write the words on the Word Wall on colorful paper with a thick, black permanent marker. Words should be placed on the wall alphabetically, and the first words added should be very different from each other. When confusing words are added, they are put on different colors of paper from the words with which they are usually confused.

Doing a Word Wall means the following:

- **Adding words gradually** (five each week)

- **Making words very accessible** by putting them where every student can see them, writing them in big, black letters, and using a variety of colors of paper so that the most often confused words (**for, from; that, them, they, this;** etc.) are written on different colors of paper

- **Being selective and stingy about which words go on the wall,** limiting additions to those words that students use a lot in writing

- **Practicing the words by chanting and writing them,** because struggling readers are not usually good visual learners and can't just look at and remember words

- **Doing a variety of review activities** to provide enough practice so that the words are read and spelled instantly and automatically

- **Making sure that the Word Wall words are spelled correctly in any student writing**

Most teachers add five new words to the wall each week and **do at least one daily** activity in which students find, write, and chant the spelling of each word. The activity takes longer on the first day that words are added, because teachers must take time to make sure that students associate meanings with the words and are not confused by any similar words.

To begin the Word Wall practice, each student numbers a sheet of paper from 1 to 5. The teacher calls out five words, pointing to each and using it in a sentence. **As the teacher calls out each word, all students clap and chant its spelling before writing it.** When students have written all five words, the teacher writes the words as students check and fix their own papers. **Many teachers include handwriting instruction with the daily Word Wall activity** and have students trace around the words to check the proper positions of the letters.

On the day new words are added, the new words are called out, clapped, chanted, and written. The week's new words are often reviewed on the second day. During the rest of the week, however, any five words from the wall can be called out. Words with which students need much practice should be called out almost every day.

On-the-Back Word Wall Activities

Early in the year, it takes the whole 10 minutes to call out, chant, write, and check five words each day. As the year goes on and writing and correct handwriting become more fluent and automatic, however, the five words can usually be written in five minutes. This leaves five minutes to do an On-the-Back activity that extends students' knowledge of the Word Wall words and/or helps them learn to spell other words.

On-the-Back Endings

This activity helps students learn how to spell Word Wall words that need endings. Imagine that these are the five Word Wall words you call out for students to locate, cheer for, and write:

| want | eat | look | talk | play |

Have students turn over their papers. Say something like the following:

"Today, we will work on how to spell these Word Wall words when they need endings. I will say some sentences like the ones many of you write, and you should listen for the Word Wall words that have had endings added."

- My friends and I love **eating** at Subway®.
- We were **looking** for some new shoes.
- I was **talking** on the phone with my friend Eva.
- My sister **wants** the new baby to be a girl.
- My friend spent the night, and we **played** games until 9 o'clock.

After each sentence, students identify the Word Wall word and the ending, decide how to spell the word, and write the word with the ending on their papers.

The example provided uses three ending—**ing**, **s**, and **ed**,—and five different words. **When first doing this activity, use fewer endings and/or fewer words**. For example, call out five words but concentrate on adding endings to only one or two of these. Imagine that **look** and **eat** are two of the five words. These could be the sentences for the On-the-Back activity:

- He **looks** hungry.
- We were **looking** for Lawrence.
- She **looked** in the bedroom.
- Andrew **eats** peanut butter sandwiches for lunch.
- We were **eating** when the fire alarm went off.

Students would have the words **looks**, **looking**, **looked**, **eats**, and **eating** written on the backs of their papers.

These endings do not require any spelling changes. Later in the year, include some words that need to have the **e** dropped, a **y** changed to an **i**, or a letter doubled. Since students decide how to spell each word before writing it, everyone spells each word correctly. This additional information about how to spell words with a variety of endings and spelling changes really moves along the accelerated learners in their writing abilities.

On-the-Back Rhymes

Another popular On-the-Back activity helps students see how some Word Wall words can help them spell a lot of other words that rhyme. **In many classrooms, teachers underline the spelling patterns and put stars or stickers by Word Wall words that share the pattern with a lot of other words.** On some days, the five words that teachers call out for students to write on the fronts of their papers are all starred or stickered words.

For the On-the-Back activity, the teacher says a sentence that contains a word that rhymes with one of the day's words and is spelled with the same pattern. Students must decide which word in this sentence rhymes and spell it. Imagine, for example, that these are the five words written on the fronts of students' papers:

| school | ride | saw | car | best |

Students turn over their papers, and the teacher asks them to listen to the following sentence for the word that rhymes with one of the words:

Sometimes, my little sister is a pest.

Students decide that **pest** rhymes with **best,** and they write **pest** next to number 1 on the backs of their papers.

The teacher continues to say sentences that are similar to what students might use in their writing, such as the following:

- My dog got a splinter in his **paw**.
- I went to a wedding because the **bride** is my aunt.
- Winter is still very **far** away.
- I swim in my neighborhood **pool**.

For each sentence, students decide which word rhymes with one of the words written on the fronts of their papers and use the spelling pattern to spell the word.

Brooke
1. school
2. ride
3. saw
4. car
5. best   **Front**

1. pest
2. claw
3. bride
4. far
5. pool   **On-the-Back**

For an easier lesson, the teacher may use only one word written on the front as the rhyming match. Imagine that the word she has called out is **ride**. She could say sentences, such as the following:

- I like to **hide** when we play hide-and-seek.

- Laura was the **bride**.

- I picked Madeline to be on my **side**.

- We saw a lot of clams at low **tide**.

- Wendell hurt his arm when he fell off the **slide**.

When doing rhyming On-the-Back activities, the teacher comes up with the rhyming words and puts them in sentences that are similar to what students might actually write. She doesn't ask students for rhyming words because there are often—particularly with the long vowels—two spelling patterns. If she asked for words that rhymed with **ride**, students might come up with **tried** and **cried**. It is important for students to learn about the two patterns, but first, they must learn that in English, we spell by pattern—not one letter for one sound.

On-the-Back Cross-Checking

To practice Cross-Checking, call out several words that begin with the same letter for students to write on the fronts of their papers, such as the following:

went	want	was	what	where

Tell students that they will decide which word makes sense in each sentence. Then, say a sentence, leaving out one of the words. Students decide which word makes sense in the sentence and write that word. Here are some possible sentences with one of the above words left out:

- They _____ to the beach.
- I _____ to go to the movies.
- It _____ very hot.
- _____ do you want to eat for dinner?
- _____ should we go first?

Be a Mind Reader

Be a Mind Reader is a favorite On-the-Back activity. **In this game, the teacher thinks of a word on the Word Wall and gives five clues about that word.**

The teacher has students number their papers from 1 to 5. He tells them that he will see who can read his mind and figure out of which word on the board he is thinking. The teacher tells students that he will give them five clues. By the fifth clue, everyone should guess the word, but if they read his mind, they might get it before the fifth clue. For the first clue, the teacher always gives the same clue:

It's one of the words on the wall.

Students should write the word that they think it might be next to number 1. Each succeeding clue should narrow down what the word might be until, by clue five, there is only one possible word.

As the teacher gives clues, each student writes the word that she believes it is next to each number on her paper. If a succeeding clue confirms the word that a student has written next to one number, then that student writes the same word next to the following number. Clues may include any features of the word that the teacher wants students to notice. For example, "It has more than two letters. It has fewer than four letters. It has an **e**. It does not have a **t**." After clue five, the teacher says, "I know that all of you have the word next to number five, but who has it next to number 4? 3? 2? 1?"

Some students will have read your mind and will be pleased with themselves!

Be a Mind Reader example:

1. It's one of the words on the wall.

2. It has four letters.

3. It begins with **wh**.

4. The vowel is **e**.

5. It begins this sentence: _____ will dinner be ready?

Phonics and Spelling

Teaching students phonics is a lot easier than teaching students to use the phonics they know. When phonics is taught in a way that is removed from reading and writing, students often learn which letters make which sounds but they are unable to quickly apply this knowledge to unfamiliar words in their reading or writing. **English is not a simple language to learn how to decode and spell. Many consonants and all of the vowels have a variety of sounds, depending on the surrounding letters.** Vowels do not have just short and long sounds.

This can be clearly understood by looking at any sentence and thinking about what the vowels do in that sentence.

In the previous sentence, for example, these words contain the vowel **o**:

| **understood** | **looking** | **about** | **vowels** | **do** |

None of these **o**'s represents the short or long sound of **o**.

In the same sentence, these words contain the vowel **e**:

| **be** | **clearly** | **understood** | **sentence** | **vowels** |

The **e** in the word **be** represents the long /e/ sound, and two of the three **e**'s in **sentence** represent the short sound of **e**. The **e** represents different sounds, not short or long, in **clearly**, **understood**, and **vowels**.

There is logic to the sounds represented by letters in English, but the logic is in the pattern, not in simple vowel rules.

Look again at the words above containing **o**. The two **o**'s in **understood** and **looking** have the same sound, and other **o-o-d** and **o-o-k** words, including **good, hood, cook,** and **shook,** share this sound. The **o-u** combination in **about** has the same sound in other **o-u-t** words, including **out, shout,** and **clout.** The **o-w** in **vowels** has the same sound in **now, how,** and **cow.** Only the **o** in **do** does not follow a predictable pattern.

Look at the patterns in **clearly**, **understood**, and **vowels**. The **e-a-r** represents the same sound as it does in **ear**, **hear**, and **dear**; the **e-r** represents the same sound as it does in **her**, **mother**, and **father**; and the **e-l** represents the same sound as it does in **towel**, **camel**, and **level**.

Phonics—the relationship between letters and sounds—makes sense in English, but only if you know to look for patterns of letters rather than at individual letters. These patterns determine the sounds for consonant letters as well as vowels. **Psychologists say that human brains separate unknown words into their onsets— all of the letters up to the first vowel—and the rimes—the first vowel and letters following the vowel.** The first time you ever saw the words **spew**, **mite**, and **phrase**, you separated their onsets (**sp**, **m**, **phr**) from their rimes (**ew**, **ite**, **ase**), and you used what you knew about consonant and vowel patterns to come up with sounds for each part and combine them. **To be good decoders and spellers, students need to learn to quickly separate words into these parts, think of sounds associated with the patterns, and combine the sounds.**

After the daily Word Wall practice, the remaining 20 minutes of Working with Words time is given to an activity that helps students learn the onset and rime patterns and how to use them to decode and spell new words. A variety of activities are used. Five of the most popular activities are described on the following pages:

- Rounding Up the Rhymes
- Making Words
- Guess the Covered Word
- Using Words You Know
- Reading/Writing Rhymes

Rounding Up the Rhymes

Rounding Up the Rhymes is a Working with Words activity that follows the reading of a selection that has a lot of rhyming words with the same spelling pattern during Guided Reading or Self-Selected Reading time.

 20 min.

Here is an example using *I Ain't Gonna Paint No More* by Karen Beaumont. Read the book once. Then, round up the rhymes! You can round up all of the rhymes in this book with second graders.

1 ### Read the Book

To do Rounding Up the Rhymes, **take the book out again during the Working with Words Block and reread several pages, focusing on the rhyming words.** Choose pages that have a lot of rhymes with the same pattern so that students will see the connection between rhyming words and spelling patterns. As you read each page, **encourage students to chime in and try to hear the rhymes that they are saying.**

2 ### Round Up the Rhymes

As students tell the rhyming words, **write them on index cards and put them in a pocket chart.** Here are some rhyming pairs rounded up:

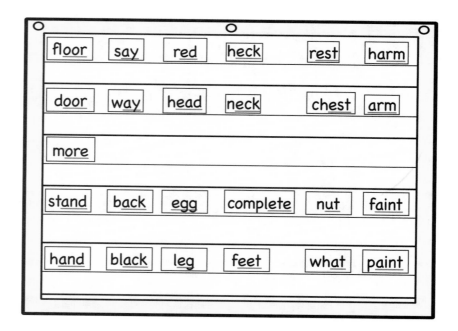

Discard the Rhymes

Next, tell students to **discard the rhymes** that don't have the same spelling patterns. The pocket chart now looks like this:

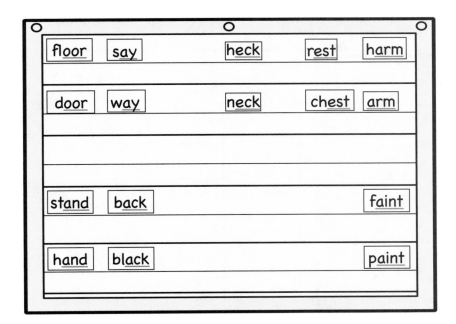

Transfer

The final part of this activity is to use these words to read and write some other words. **This is the transfer step, and it is critical to the success of this activity** for students who learn only what you teach. Begin the transfer part of the activity by telling students something like this:

"You know that when you are reading books and writing stories, there are many words you have never seen before. You have to figure them out. One way that many people figure out how to read and spell new words is to see if they already know any rhyming words, or words that have the same spelling patterns. I will write some words, and you can see which words with the same spelling pattern will help you read each word I've written. Then, we will try to spell some words by deciding whether they rhyme with any of the words in our pocket chart."

Write a word—**clay**—that rhymes with and has the same spelling pattern as some of the rounded-up rhymes. Without letting students pronounce the word, have someone put it with the rhyming words in the pocket chart. Once **clay** is placed under **say** and **way**, have the class pronounce all three words. Do this reading transfer with another word—**test**. Then, do the spelling transfer by saying a couple of words—**crack** and **charm**, and having students decide with which words they rhyme and then use the rhymes to spell them. At the end of the activity, the rounded-up rhymes and the transfer words are lined up in the pocket chart.

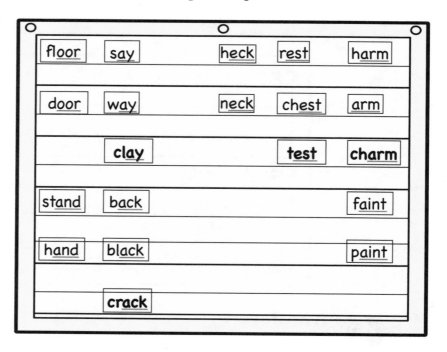

Rounding Up the Rhymes is a great Working with Words activity to follow the reading of any book that has several pages on which there are rhyming words with the same spelling pattern. **Having the rhymes come from a book and doing some transfer rhymes increases the probability that students will actually use rhyming words they know as they encounter new words in their reading and as they need to spell words while writing.** Rounding Up the Rhymes is an appropriate activity to do when most students have developed the ability to hear rhymes and are ready to see how rhyming patterns work.

Other good books with a lot of rhyming words include the following:

The Best Vacation Ever by Stuart J. Murphy (HarperTrophy, 1997)

Birds Build Nests by Yvonne Winer (Charlesbridge Publishing, 2002)

The Brand New Kid by Katie Couric (Doubleday, 2000)

The Crayon Box That Talked by Shane DeRolf (Random House, 1997)

The Flea's Sneeze by Lynn Downey (Turtleback, 2005)

The Grumpy Morning by Pamela Duncan Edwards (Hyperion, 1998)

Loud Lips Lucy by Tolya L. Thompson (Savor Publishing, 2001)

More Parts by Tedd Arnold (Puffin Books, 2003)

The Ten Best Things about My Dad by Christine Loomis (Scholastic Paperback, 2004)

Somewhere in the Ocean by Jennifer Ward (Rising Moon, 2000)

Making Words

20 min.

Making Words (Cunningham & Hall, 1994; Cunningham & Hall, 1997) is an active, hands-on, manipulative activity in which students learn how to look for patterns in words and how changing just one letter changes a whole word. Students are given six to eight letters that will form a final secret word. The lesson begins with small words, builds to longer words, and finally ends with the secret word that can be made with all of the letters. Then, students sort the words according to a variety of patterns, such as beginning sounds, endings, and rhymes. They transfer the patterns by using the sorted words to read and spell words with similar patterns.

For this example lesson, each student has five consonant cards—**d**, **p**, **r**, **s**, and **s**—and two vowel cards—**e** and **i**. In the pocket chart at the front of the room, the teacher has large cards with the same seven letters. Each of her cards, like the small letter cards used by students, has the uppercase letter on one side and lowercase letter on the other side. The consonant letters are written in black and the two vowels are in red. (See page 140 for detailed steps in planning a Making Words lesson.)

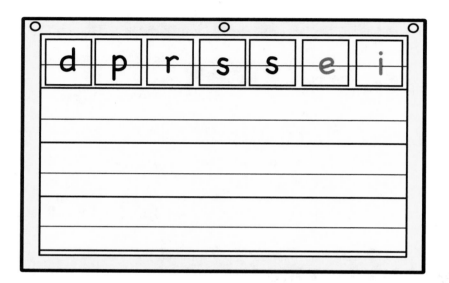

 ### Make Step

The teacher begins by making sure that each student has all of the letters that are needed. "What two vowels will we use to make words today?" she asks. Students hold up the red **e** and **i** cards. Students then name the consonants. The teacher writes the number 3 on the board and says:

"The first three-letter word that I want you to make today is a word that you already know: **red**."

She sends someone who has quickly spelled **red** to the pocket chart to make **red** with the big letters and to put an index card with the word **red** written on it in the chart. She then gives this direction:

"Just change your vowel, and you can change **red** to **rid**. Sometimes, I ask you to clean out your desks and get **rid** of the junk."

Next, she writes a 4 on the board and says, "Add just one letter to **rid** to make the four-letter word **ride**."

The lesson continues with students making each word with their individual letter cards, followed by a student going to the pocket chart to make the word and put the index-card word in the chart.

The teacher does not wait for everyone to make the word before sending someone to the pocket chart, and some students are still making their words as the word is being made with the pocket-chart letters. Before making another word, the teacher reminds students to fix their words to match the one made with the big letters.

Directed by the teacher, students change **ride** to **side**. Then, they do an "abracadabra" in which they move around the letters in **side** to spell **dies**. They change the first letter in **dies** to spell **pies**.

The teacher writes a 5 on the board and says, "Add a letter to **pies** to spell **pries**. 'The boy **pries** open the top of the rusty, old box.'"

Pries is changed to **dries** and then to **spies**. Then, the teacher gives this direction:

"Change one letter to change **spies** to **spied**. 'She **spied** a quarter in a dusty corner.' Now, change **spied** to **pried**. 'It took a lot of work, but finally, they **pried** open the door.'"

Next, the teacher tells students that they can do another abracadabra and turn the **pried** that means "forced open" into the **pride** that she is always telling them they need to take in their work. Then, they make two more five-letter words, **press** and **dress**.

Finally, the teacher says, "I don't have any six-letter words for you today, so I am coming around to see who has the secret word."

She gives students one minute, and several students have figured out the secret word, **spiders**. She sends one student to make **spiders** with the big letters and put the index-card word **spiders** in the pocket chart.

Sort Step

After making the words, it is time to sort for patterns and use those patterns to read and spell a few new words. The teacher has students read all of the words that they have made, which are now displayed in the pocket chart:

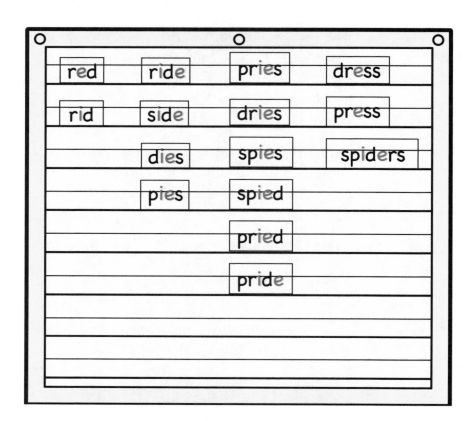

She then has students pull out and line up the words that rhyme and have the same spelling pattern:

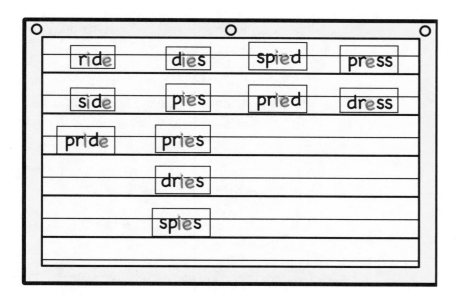

3 Transfer Step

The final step of every Making Words lesson is the transfer step. Once the rhymes are sorted, the teacher shows students an index card on which the word **chess** is written:

"What if you were reading, came to this word, and didn't know it? Don't say this word even if you know it. Who can put this word with the rhyming words that will help you figure it out?"

A student places **chess** under the other **e-s-s** words, and all students pronounce **chess**. Next, the teacher says:

"I have two more words that you might not immediately know if you came to them in your reading."

She shows them cards on which she has written **glide** and **fried**. Students place these words under the rhyming words with the same patterns and pronounce them.

The teacher then explains that students can use rhyming patterns to help them in writing too.

"Thinking of words that rhyme helps you when you are trying to spell a word too. What if you were writing and needed to spell **ties**? Which rhyming words would help you?"

Students decide that **ties** rhymes with **dies**, **pies**, **pries**, **dries**, and **spies** and would probably be spelled **t-i-e-s**.

The teacher helps students notice the two spelling patterns **i-e-d** and **i-d-e** for the same rhyme:

"When there are two spelling patterns for the same rhyme, we usually have to pick the one that looks right, ask for help, or look in the dictionary to see which way to spell it. For these spelling patterns, though, there is a clue you can use: think about related words."

The teacher writes the words **spy**, **pry**, and **fry** next to **spied**, **pried**, and **fried**. Students talk about how the words are related and how **y** is changed to **i** when adding **ed**.

"I will say a word that rhymes with **ride**, **side**, **pride**, and **slide** and also with **spied**, **pried**, and **fried**. If you think about its related word, you can probably figure out which pattern it is spelled with. The word is **cried**. 'The baby **cried** all night.' How do you think you would spell **cried**?"

Several students' hands wave enthusiastically, and they are proud to explain that the word would be spelled **c-r-i-e-d** because the related word is **cry** and **y** is changed to **i**. (If your students are not at the stage where they could understand this **i-e-d** /**i-d-e** distinction and you want to do the **spiders** lesson, simply have them make two other words, such as **dip** and **drip**, instead of **spied** and **pried**.)

Writing Transfer

The teacher asks students to take out a piece of paper or passes out half sheets of paper and tells them to write these five words: **slide**, **tried**, **bless**, **hide**, and **cries**.

4 Homework Sheet

For homework, students have the Making Words homework sheet. The letters **e**, **i**, **d**, **p**, **r**, **s**, and **s** are in boxes along the top, and there are larger boxes below in which students should write words. They should cut apart the letters, write uppercase letters on the backs, and fill the boxes with words they can make with the letters, including some words they made in class.

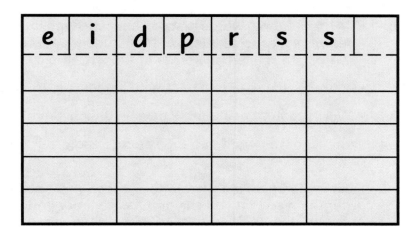

Several students comment when they bring back the sheets the next day that they showed their parents how words with both patterns, **i-e-d** and **i-d-e**, rhyme. They explained that they can figure out how to spell words if they think about related words, like **cry** and **cried**. They then pointed out that it worked for **try** and **tried** and **dry** and **dried** too. Their pride in their word wizardry is evident!

Steps in Planning a Making Words Lesson

1. Decide upon a secret word that can be made with all of the letters. In choosing this word, consider student interest, the curriculum tie-ins that you can make, and the letter-sound patterns to which you can draw students' attention through the sorting step.

2. Make a list of other words that can be made from these letters.

3. From all of the words you could make, pick 12–15 words using these criteria:

   • Words that you can sort for the pattern you want to emphasize

   • Little words and big words so that the lesson is a multilevel lesson (Making little words helps struggling students; making big words challenges your highest-achieving students.)

   • "Abracadabra" words that can be made with the same letters in different places (**side/dies**) so that students are reminded that when words are spelled, the order of the letters is crucial

   • A proper name or two to remind students to use uppercase letters

   • Words that most students have in their listening vocabularies

4. Write all of the words on index cards and order them from shortest to longest.

5. Once you have the two-letter, three-letter, etc., words together, order them so that you can emphasize letter patterns and show how changing the position of the letters, changing one letter, or adding one letter results in a different word.

6. Choose some letters or patterns by which to sort.

7. Choose four transfer words—uncommon words you can read and spell based on the rhyming words.

8. Store the cards in an envelope. On the envelope, write the words in order, the patterns by which you will sort, and the transfer words.

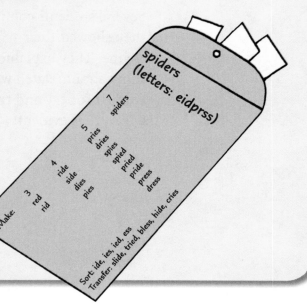

spiders
(letters: eidprss)

Make:
3 red rid
4 ride side dies pies
5 pries dries spies spied pride press dress
7 spiders

Sort: ide, ies, ied, ess
Transfer: slide, tried, bless, hide, cries

Guess the Covered Word

Guess the Covered Word is another popular Working with Words activity. **Its purpose is to help students practice the important strategy of cross-checking meaning with letter-sound information.** Here is the procedure:

The teacher writes four or five sentences on the board, covering a word in each sentence with two sticky notes—one covering the onset, which is all of the consonants prior to the first vowel, and the other sticky note covering the rest of the word. Most teachers tear their sticky notes so that students also become sensitive to word length.

Students read each sentence and make several guesses for the covered word. (The teacher points out that there are generally many possibilities for a word that will fit the context when you can't see any of the letters.) The guesses are written on the board.

Next, the teacher takes off the first sticky note, which always covers all of the letters up to the vowel.

Guesses that don't begin with these letters are erased or crossed out, and new guesses that both fit the meaning and start with the right beginning letters are made.

When all of the guesses that fit both the meaning and the beginning sounds have been written, the whole word is revealed.

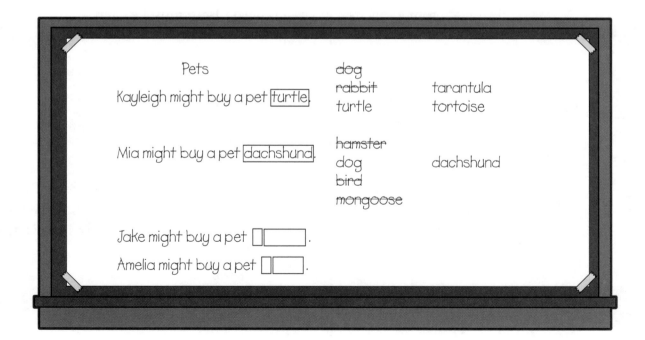

20 min.

Using Words You Know

There are hundreds of spelling patterns commonly found in one- and two-syllable words. **A good reader figures out a new word by looking at the spelling pattern and thinking of other words with that pattern.** To spell a new word, a good reader thinks of a rhyming word and tries that pattern to see if it looks right. If it doesn't look right, he thinks of another word that rhymes but has a different spelling pattern. **Using Words You Know is an activity that helps students learn to use the words they can read and spell to read and spell hundreds of other words.** Here is the procedure:

To plan a Using Words You Know lesson, pick three or four words that your students know that have many rhyming words spelled the same way. You can use high-frequency words, such as **big, play,** and **not.** You can also use color words, number words, vehicle words, food words, animal words, or seasonal words—any words that your students know that have a lot of rhyming words. For this example lesson, we will use the number words **ten, nine,** and **five.**

Using the board or overhead, make three columns and head them with the key words. Have each student do the same on a sheet of paper. Tell students that you will show them a word that rhymes with **ten, nine,** or **five.** When you show them the word, have them write it in the column under the rhyming word. Then, have them use the rhyming word to decode the new word. Have them verbalize the strategy that they are using by saying something like "If **t-e-n** is **ten, G-l-e-n** must be **Glen.**"

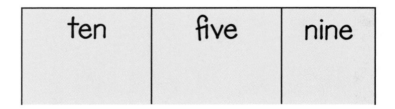

ten	five	nine

Write **Glen** under **ten** in your column and show them the next word. Do not let anyone say the word until they have written it in the correct column. Have them verbalize their strategy as they tell you the word: "If **f-i-v-e** is **five, d-r-i-v-e** is **drive.**"

After you have shown students several words and they have used the known words to decode them, help them practice using known words to spell unknown words. This time, say a word, such as **shine**, and have students write it under the word with which it rhymes. Have them verbalize how they spelled **shine** by leading them to explain, "If **nine** is spelled **n-i-n-e**, **shine** is probably spelled **s-h-i-n-e**."

For these lessons, be sure that you tell students what rhyming words to spell instead of having them come up with the words. In English, there are often two spelling patterns for the same rhyme. If you ask them what rhymes with **three**, they are apt to come up with words with the **e** pattern, such as **me** and **he**. So, for this strategy, you supply the words that rhyme and choose only rhymes with the same spelling pattern.

You can plan Using Words You Know lessons quickly and easily by using a rhyming dictionary. Here are some words that rhyme with and have the same spelling patterns as **ten, nine,** and **five**:

ten	five	nine
Glen	dive	shine
wren	drive	pine
hen	jive	spine
men	hive	fine
then	strive	line
when		mine
Ben		whine
		vine

Reading/Writing Rhymes

Reading/Writing Rhymes is an activity that gives students practice using patterns to decode and spell hundreds of words. Once all of the rhyming words are generated on a chart, students write rhymes using these words and read each other's rhymes. Because reading and writing are connected to every lesson, students learn how to use these patterns as they actually read and write. Here is an example of how one Reading/Writing Rhymes lesson might be carried out:

The teacher has distributed the whole set of beginning-letter cards (see list below) to students. Because there are more onsets than students, most students have two cards. The index cards are laminated and have **single-letter consonant onsets written in blue, the blends in red, and the digraphs and other two-letter combinations in green**. On one side of each card, the first letter of the onset is an uppercase letter. In passing out the cards, the teacher has considered the levels of her students. Students who are still learning single-consonant onsets are given these. The most advanced students are given the less-common, more-complex onsets, such as **str** and **ph**.

The onset deck contains 50 beginning-letter cards, including these:

Single consonants in blue:
b c d f g h j k l m n p r s t v w y z

Digraphs (two letters, one sound) in green: ch kn ph qu sh th wh wr

Blends (beginning letters blended together, also called clusters) in red:
bl br cl cr dr fl fr gl gr pl pr sc scr sk sl sm sn sp spr st str sw tr

To make instruction as nonjargony as possible, refer to all of these cards as beginning-letter cards. Students learn that when they are trying to figure out how to read or spell a word, they should use all of the letters up to the vowel. Some schools demand that students learn the terminology. Terms such as *consonants, blends, digraphs, clusters,* etc., are confusing to many students and can actually interfere with their learning how to use letters and sounds. The terminology is included here. Do not use it with your students unless they will be penalized for not knowing it. **Regardless of what you call it, try to ensure that all of your students learn that when trying to read or spell a new word, they should use all of the letters up to the first vowel and then look at the spelling pattern—the rest of the word.**

Once all of the onset cards are distributed, the teacher writes the spelling pattern eight times on a piece of chart paper. As she writes it each time, she has students help spell and pronounce it.

Next, the teacher invites students who have onsets that they think will make words with the pattern to come to the chart. Then, each student places the card next to one of the written spelling patterns and pronounces the word. If the word is a real word, the teacher uses the word in a sentence and writes that word on the chart. If the word is not a real word, she explains why she cannot write it on the chart. (If a word is a real word and does rhyme but has a different spelling pattern, such as **planned** to rhyme with **and**, the teacher explains that it rhymes but has a different spelling pattern, and she includes it on the bottom of the chart with an asterisk next to it.) The teacher writes names with uppercase letters, and if a word can be both a name and not a name, such as **Jack** and **jack**, she writes it both ways.

When all students who think they can spell words by adding their beginning letters to the spelling pattern have had turns, the teacher calls students to make the words not yet on the chart. She says something like "I think that the person with the **wh** card could add **wh** to **ack** to make a word we know."

The teacher tries to include all words that any students have in their listening vocabularies but avoids obscure words. If all eight patterns on the chart have been made into complete words, she adds as many words as needed. Finally, if the class can think of some good longer words that rhyme and have that spelling pattern, the teacher adds them. Of course, since students don't have all of the letters to spell these longer words, the teacher just writes these on the list.

3 Once the chart of rhyming words is written, the class works together in a shared writing format to write a silly rhyme using a lot of the rhyming words.

The cop went to shop at the Stop and Shop for a mop.

4 Next, students write rhymes of their own. Many teachers put together small groups or partner students to write these rhymes and then let students read their rhymes to the class.

Don't stop or hop, but mop the drop so that we can shop at the Stop and Shop and see if there is a new crop.

Clop, clop went the horse.
Hop, hop went the rabbit.
Stop, stop said Pop.
I will drop my mop if you don't stop.

Zack went back to see Mr. Mack when he heard a quack near the track. There sat Jack with a backpack sitting on a crack with his snack.

Jack and Mack ate a snack from his backpack.
They packed the snack to eat at the black shack near the racetrack.

When the class has made several charts, the teacher reviews with students all of the rhyming words on the charts and lets students write rhymes using words from all of the charts. Many teachers let each student pick one rhyme to edit and illustrate, and they compile class books of rhymes for everyone to read and enjoy.

Order of Lessons

You can make the charts in any order. Some teachers like to make all of the short /a/ charts first, talk about the sound that **a** makes in all of these words, and then make charts for the other short vowels. Other teachers like to do all of the different sounds for **a** and then move on to the other vowels. If you are using a basal reader or curriculum guide that specifies an order in which the vowel sounds will be taught and tested, let that order determine the order in which you make charts for Reading/Writing Rhymes.

Just as for Using Words You Know, use a rhyming dictionary, such as the *Scholastic Rhyming Dictionary* by Sue Young, as a source for rhyming words. Pick the patterns that have the most rhyming examples. Some patterns will generate some "bad words." You can choose not to distribute the onsets that would make these words. Or, tell students that there are some words that could be made but that "we never use in school," so you won't include them. (You don't need anyone to tell you what they are!)

Suggested Short Vowel Patterns for Reading/Writing Rhymes

For the short vowels, these are the most common rhyming patterns:

a:	ack	ad	am	an	and	ap	ash	at
e:	ed	ell	en	et	est			
i:		ick	id	ill	in	ip	it	
o:	ob	ock	op	ot				
u:	uck	ug	ump	unch	unk	ut		

The other most common vowel sounds are sometimes called the long sounds. Some students find it easier to figure out these long vowel words because they can actually hear the vowel "saying its name." Again, don't confuse students by placing too much emphasis on the terminology or the rules. Rather, have them notice the patterns.

The easiest and most consistent long vowel spelling for **a** is the **a-y** pattern, so begin with that one, using the same procedure of handing out all 50 beginning-letter cards. Invite students who have onsets that they think will make real words with the pattern to come to the chart, place their cards next to **ay**, say the words, and use the words in sentences. When students have not noticed that their letters will make words, give them clues by saying something like "I think that the person who has the **br** could spell the word that is the sound that a donkey makes."

Just as for short vowels, finish by adding to the chart longer **ay** words that rhyme, along with any common rhyming words with different spelling patterns. Students are always amazed at how many wonderful rhyming words there are on the **ay** chart and eagerly write a lot of silly rhymes.

_ ay

day	today	pray	holiday
say	Monday	pay	faraway
way	Tuesday	way	subway
play	Wednesday	tray	*sleigh
lay	Thursday	Ray	*weigh
bay	Friday	ray	*hey
hay	Saturday	sway	*they
may	Sunday	slay	*ballet
May	birthday	bray	*croquet
stay	away	spray	
stray	highway		
clay	X-ray		
gray	yesterday		

* Some words sound right but are not spelled the correct way.

The second most common way of spelling the long /a/ sound is with an **a**, a consonant, and then a silent **e**. A good way to introduce this is with the **a-k-e** pattern, because it has many rhyming words. The other common combination for the long /a/ sound is **a-i**.

Many rhyming words can be spelled with **a-(consonant)-e** or **a-i**. The fact that there are two common patterns is not a problem when reading. Students quickly learn that both **a-(consonant)-e** and **a-i** often have the long /a/ sound. When a student is spelling a word, however, he has no way of knowing which one is the correct spelling, unless he recognizes it as a word he knows after writing it. This is why people often write a word, think, "That doesn't look right," and try writing it with another pattern to see if that looks right.

When writing rhymes that have two common spelling patterns, the teacher should write both patterns on the same chart. Students tell the words that their beginning letters will make with the patterns, and the teacher writes each word with the correct pattern. In many cases, there are homophones, words that have the same pronunciation but are spelled differently and have different meanings. The teacher writes both of these words and talks about what each one means. An artistic teacher draws a little picture next to one of the words so that students can tell the homophones apart. Here is the chart for the **a-i-l/a-l-e** long vowel spelling patterns:

_ ail / _ ale			
fail	sail	sale	scale
mail	tail	tale	male
trail	wail	whale	Dale
snail	pail	pale	tattletale
frail	Gail	gale	wholesale
hail	cottontail	Yale	female
bail	quail	stale	
nail	jail		
detail	monorail		
toenail	rail		

Here are the long vowel combinations that have the most examples for rhyming patterns:

a:	aid/ade	ail/ale	ain/ane	ait/ate	ake
e:	ead/eed	eal/eel	eat/eet		
i:	ice	ide	ine	ite/ight	
o:	o/oe	oan/one	oke/oak	old	ote/oat ow
u:	ute/oot				

All of the common vowel patterns can be taught through Reading/Writing Rhymes. Always choose the patterns that will generate the most rhymes. When there is more than one common spelling for a rhyme, include both—or in some cases, all three—spelling patterns. Here are the other vowel sounds that are common enough to merit teaching:

The R-Vowel Patterns:

ar	ark	art
are (care)/air	ear (near)/ere/eer	
ert/irt/urt	irl/url	urn/ern/earn
orn	ort	ore/oar

The special sounds of the vowel **a** when it is followed by **l, u,** or **w:**

aw	all	awl	aul

Some people consider the **a-n-k, a-n-g, i-n-k,** and **i-n-g** patterns to be long vowels, and some people consider them to be short vowels. In many dialects, they are somewhere between these long and short sounds. In any case, they are common enough that students should learn them.

ank	ang	ink	ing

O is the vowel with the most sounds. Reading/Writing Rhymes charts might be made for these:

ook	ood	oom	ool
oy	oil	out	ow (how)
ew/ue/oo (too)			

The letter **y** functions as a vowel in some words. Here is a chart for its most common sounds:

_ y	
my	* eye
by	* rye
sky	* good-bye
spy	* die
sly	* tie
why	* lie
dry	* pie
fry	* buy
fly	* guy
try	
sty	
pry	
butterfly	
defy	* Some words sound right but are not spelled the same way.
deny	
reply	
apply	
rely	
qualify	
satisfy	
multiply	

Decoding and Spelling Variations

Decoding and spelling activities that occur in the 20 minutes of Working with Words following Word Wall every day vary depending on the needs of students, the personality of the teacher, the grade level, and the time of year. If the teacher tries to make each of these activities as multilevel as possible, there is not as much variance for the grade level and the time of year as might be expected.

First-grade teachers generally spend a lot of time with phonemic awareness activities that help students learn to segment and blend words and to deal with the concept of rhyme. Teachers should continue to include some work with phonemic awareness throughout second grade because many students require a lot of varied practice with this before they truly understand it.

Rounding Up the Rhymes

Rounding Up the Rhymes is an activity that can be used numerous times throughout the primary grades. The procedures are the same, but the books from which the class is working and the rhyming patterns are different each time.

Making Words

Teachers should use fewer letters and only one vowel in early Making Words lessons. From the five letters **i, k, n, s,** and **t,** for example, the class might make the words **in, it, sit, kit, kin, skin, sink,** and **stink.** Even in these early lessons, students should sort for patterns and use sorted rhyming words to read and spell some transfer words.

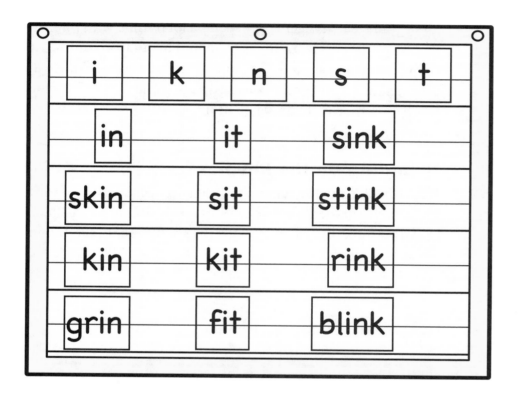

In the example lesson above, the words were first sorted according to initial letters and then into rhyming words. These rhyming words were used to figure out how to decode **fit** and **grin** and how to spell **rink** and **blink.**

Guess the Covered Word

Teachers should only cover words with single-consonant onsets in the first Guess the Covered Word lessons but soon include words that begin with letter combinations, such as **sh** and **br**. They should never completely move away from including some words with single initial consonants, however.

For the first lessons, only words at the ends of sentences are covered. Later, covered words occur anywhere in the sentences. Teachers can also do some lessons in which the covered words occur in paragraphs taken from stories or informational books.

Using Words You Know

Using Words You Know lessons can be used to teach any vowel patterns. They are perfect for second grade. Second graders can read many easy words and use these words they know to read and spell many other words. For example, they know color words (*red, green, black, brown,* etc.), number words (*five, ten, three, nine,* etc.), animal names (*dog, cat, pig, goat,* etc.), vehicle names (*car, truck, van, bike,* etc.), and people's names (*Dan, Zach, Pat,* etc.). When reading a selection in Guided Reading, look for easy words with patterns that can lead your students to read and write many more words.

Reading/Writing Rhymes

Reading/Writing Rhymes is most effective in second and third grades. Teachers choose the patterns depending on which phonics and spelling principles their students need to learn or review.

Frequently Asked Questions

Q: Do all students need all four blocks?

A: No, but all classrooms full of students do!

Some students seem equally engaged and successful in each block. These students would probably learn to read no matter what approach was used. Other students have clearly observable preferences, and if you watch closely, you can almost see them "click in" during the block that matches their learning personality. We have watched students in hundreds of classrooms learn to read within the Four-Blocks framework. **In every classroom, we can identify students who would not learn to read as well if any block were eliminated.**

Q: What happens to students in Four-Blocks classrooms who would otherwise be in the bottom group?

A: They do better than they did when we had them in the bottom group!

While we use many grouping formats for our instruction, we don't have fixed reading groups. Thus, students have no sense of being in a top, middle, or bottom group. Second-graders who come to school with little print experience but much eagerness to learn maintain their eagerness and their "I can do anything" attitude. Many of our inexperienced second-graders learn to read and write at grade level or better.

Previously, when we put students in the bottom group, we combined two types of learners: slow learners and inexperienced learners. When slow learners and inexperienced learners are combined, the pace of learning is slowed and the opportunity to learn is limited. In contrast, when inexperienced, but fast, learners are given multiple opportunities to read and write and don't become discouraged by low-group placement, they make up for lost time.

The bottom group is usually the most diverse. It is more difficult to meet their needs by lumping them into one group than by using different formats based on individual, partner, and small-group activities. We began with the theory that grouping students was not the best solution to the problems presented by the varying reading levels of students entering school. Our abstract idea has now been replaced with the measurable success of real kid readers and writers.

Q: Do students who would have been in the top group get enough challenging reading on their levels?

A: There is never enough, but they get more than they did when we had them in the top group.

When our students were divided into reading groups, the top group in any grade level usually received reading material just slightly above grade level. This modification was not enough to accelerate the achievement of the best readers. However, in the Four-Blocks framework, students spend half of their time in the Self-Selected Reading and Writing Blocks, in which there is no limit to the level at which they can read and write. With no limits on how fast they can learn, our best readers astonish us year after year. **It is clear that reading groups were as limiting for students in the top group as they were for students in the bottom group.**

Q: What do you do about worksheets?

A: Worksheets are used as little as possible.

The number of worksheets completed during the Four-Blocks time is minimal. We don't need worksheets to keep students busy. Another reason is that how well students read directly correlates to how much time they spend actually reading and writing. Finally, worksheets are often a poor use of students' reading and writing time, particularly for students who read above or below grade level. For a worksheet to help students improve in reading, it must meet three criteria:

- **First, the worksheet must require that the student read and/or write.** This may seem obvious, but consider some of the worksheets given to students in primary grades. For example, as part of an animals unit, students might complete a connect-the-dots worksheet and color the lion they created. Next, they might cut out and paste on additional body parts to create a new animal. While these worksheets are thematically connected to the unit, they involve minimal—if any—reading and writing. Therefore, time spent on these worksheets cannot possibly move students forward in reading and writing.

- **The second criterion is that students must be able to complete the worksheet with an 80% to 85% level of success.** Most struggling readers can usually achieve that level of success only by getting their answers from classmates on the way to the pencil sharpener!

- **Third, students must actually need practice in the strategy or skill that the worksheet reinforces.** This criterion, when met, ensures that worksheets will be a productive use of time for above-average readers. Most of the best readers in any classroom can complete a worksheet perfectly in less than 10 minutes. They and their parents are happy to see the perfect papers and stickers they bring home, but if the worksheet reinforces a strategy that students can already do fluently and without thought, they haven't grown by completing it.

Worksheets are not multilevel. Struggling readers can't do them, while high achievers don't need them. Students' reading achievement correlates highly with how they use every minute of their time. Worksheets are seldom worth the time. **Occasionally, we do use worksheet activities to practice important skills. We often partner students so that struggling readers can successfully complete worksheets. We use some worksheets to add to our assessment portfolios.** Overall, however, worksheets are a minimal part of Four-Blocks instructional time.

Q: **How do you get it all done?**

A: We don't try to "add it on" and still do everything else.

The Four-Blocks framework is used to organize all aspects of reading instruction; it is not added on to what the teacher is currently doing.

- The basal or traditional reading instruction is done during the Guided Reading Block.

- Writing becomes a part of the Writing Block and is done in the writers' workshop format.

- Grammar and language skills are taught during the Writing Block.

- Spelling and phonics are taught in the Working with Words Block.

- DEAR (Drop Everything And Read) is incorporated in the Self-Selected Reading Block.

Many of the blocks are familiar to teachers. Making the blocks multilevel is sometimes new, but that is not an add-on.

Q: **How do you give grades?**

A: **With fear and trepidation!**

As teachers think about implementing Four Blocks in their classrooms, they often worry about this question the most. We do not have a totally satisfactory answer, because we believe that the concept of giving grades—at least in primary grades—is not realistic. Grades are based on the notion that students all begin at the same place and that those who work hard will get their just reward, while those who don't will be punished with bad grades. In primary grades, however, this is not how things work. **Students come to us on different levels. If we grade them by comparing each student to everyone else, the struggling readers will fail—not because they don't try, but because of where they started. The high achievers will get wonderful grades—again, not because they are working hard, but because of where they started.**

Most teachers in Four-Blocks classrooms are required to give grades, and they do. **These teachers try to ensure that students' grades reflect their growth. They communicate with parents about the student's starting point, as well as the growth.** Teachers indicate whether a student is reading at, below, or above grade level. They include comments about specific strategies on which the student is working. They justify grades with work samples—first-draft writing, published pieces, tape-recorded readings, running records, written responses to Guided Reading selections, logs of books read during Self-Selected Reading, and occasional worksheets.

The true purpose of grades and report cards is to inform students and their parents about students' learning and progress. Teachers in Four-Blocks classrooms accompany letter grades with comments about students' reading level, effort, and progress. Struggling students who put forth effort do not get failing grades. Achieving readers get A's only for putting effort toward continued growth—not for simply having started at a higher level.

Q: How do students with special educational needs fit into Four-Blocks classrooms?

A: They fit in better than they did in more traditional classrooms!

Both classroom teachers and special education teachers who have taught in traditional, ability-grouped classrooms consistently tell us that their students' special educational needs can be more easily met within the Four-Blocks framework.

Q: Can you use ability grouping in a Four-Blocks classroom?

A: We do not recommend it.

A basic tenet of Four-Blocks instruction is not to put students in fixed ability groups. There are many reasons for this. Students placed in the bottom group often perceive themselves as poor readers and act accordingly. The bottom and top group contains an inordinate number of students with attention and behavioral problems, and it is difficult to keep them all focused and on task. Furthermore, there are always differences in reading levels within the bottom group. Yet, instruction tends to be geared toward either the highest or lowest end and does not address the needs of the other end.

Four-Blocks instruction is not ability-grouped, nor is it whole-class instruction in the grade-level books. We are concerned with providing instructional-level reading for all students, but we make our instruction multilevel in many ways in each block. We do not believe that Guided Reading is the only way to teach students to read. Some students struggle with Guided Reading but become readers because of the instruction the teacher provides during the other blocks.

Q: How do you do everything in the basal manual in a 30- to 40-minute Guided Reading Block?

A: We don't.

We are choosy about which activities we do during Guided Reading, and we do some activities during the other blocks. Because basals are designed to meet a wide spectrum of student and curricular needs, they offer far more activities than any one teacher should or could ever use. **Teachers must use their professional judgment to select appropriate activities for their students.**

- We use the basals' comprehension strategy lessons if they provide good instruction.

- We introduce some, but not all, of the suggested vocabulary. Although, we are much more apt to introduce it through picture walks and other book-connected activities than through charts.

- If the basals include sight words, phonics, and spelling skills that we deem worthwhile, we teach these during the Working with Words Block. We teach these word skills in ways we consider more active and more multilevel than the activities suggested in most basal manuals.

- If the basals include writing skills—punctuation, paragraphs, etc.—we work on them during the mini-lesson part of our Writing Block.

The Guided Reading Block is done with and without basal readers. Often, we use the adopted basal along with multiple copies of favorite children's books. **Whether we use basals or other books during this block, we concentrate on comprehension strategies, development of vocabulary and word meaning, prior knowledge, and reading and rereading for fluency.** In Four-Blocks classrooms, we try to "do it all" instructionally, but that does not include doing all of the activities in the basal manual.

 Q: **Is there a single best order in which to do the Four Blocks?**

A: **No.**

Once teachers decide on a schedule that works best for them, they usually do the same blocks at the same times each day, but they can be done in any order. Teachers have many reasons for scheduling certain blocks when they do. Some teachers do their favorite block first thing in the morning to get the day off to a great start. Other teachers schedule their least favorite block first to get it out of the way.

In some classrooms, a special teacher, an assistant, or another helper comes for part of the day. Many teachers feel that Guided Reading and Writing are the two blocks that benefit most from having an extra adult in the classroom, and thus, they schedule one or both of these blocks for times when they will have help.

We would prefer that teachers schedule their time so that students who leave for special instruction will not miss any blocks unless teachers are absolutely certain those students will receive instruction in that approach while out of the classroom. If a student goes to Reading Recovery, for example, that student is getting the very best Guided Reading instruction, so teachers might schedule the classroom Guided Reading Block during that time. Another possibility is for the Reading Recovery teacher to vary the times when students are taken out so that they do not miss the same block every day.

Generally, it is best to schedule blocks when all students are there. Sometimes, this necessitates scheduling one or more blocks in the afternoon. This actually works out well for some students who are not "morning people."

How You Can Help Your Child

- Talk about books with your child. Ask what he or she has read in school. Look for books that your child will bring home, and read *to* your child, read *with your* child, or simply *listen* as he or she reads. (The teacher will let you know which way is appropriate for your child.)

- Frequently share something that you're reading—books, newspapers, recipes, magazines, etc.— with your child to let him or her know that you value reading. Do the same with writing. When you write a note or letter, share it and talk about it with your child. Seeing their parents as readers and writers really makes an impression on children.

- Get a library card for your child at the public library, if possible, and visit on a regular basis.

- Consider giving your child a choice at bedtime: "Would you like for me to turn out the light, or would you like to read a book for 10 minutes?"

- Keep reading and writing materials available for your child.

- Read aloud to your child, even after he or she learns to read. Reading aloud should continue at least through elementary school.

- Try to attend school events, such as Open House and conferences with your child's teacher. We want to be partners in your child's education.

Did You Know?

Research supports the idea that the single most important activity for building the knowledge required for eventual success in reading is reading aloud to students.

(cited from *Becoming a Nation of Readers*)

How Your Child Will Succeed at Reading and Writing This Year

Our school believes that students who are good readers and writers will be better, happier students and citizens. We have made a commitment to do all that we can to ensure that all of our students will be good readers and writers. Because our school recognizes that all students learn differently, we know that we must find ways to reach students no matter what their strengths and weaknesses might be. Our teachers are using a method of instruction called the Four-Blocks® Model, and we want to tell you about it. We also want to ask that you play an important part in helping us with the development of your child as a reader and writer.

There are four basic ways that students have always learned to read. Usually, a school or teacher would choose one of those methods in the hopes of reaching most students. The Four-Blocks Model, however, allows us to reach all students by teaching all four methods every day.

The Four-Blocks method has proven to be quite effective for the schools that implement it, and our teachers have worked hard to learn to use this method. We have four blocks of time devoted to learning to read and write during the day. In this pamphlet, we describe what you might expect to see in the classroom during each block of language arts time. We invite you to come and visit to see how your child is learning and growing.

Guided Reading Block

During this block of time, we focus on reading comprehension skills—those strategies that help readers make sense of the print on the page. We also work on reading fluency—the smoothness with which we read text.

The teacher directs a lesson about a particular story or text. Next, students will read the selection, often in pairs or small groups. Then, the teacher will again work with the whole group of students to discuss what they have learned. Students will get a great deal of support from their teacher and classmates. They will work toward becoming independent readers.

Self-Selected Reading Block

During this block, students will have an opportunity to see themselves as readers and to build their fluency, or ability to read smoothly. The block will begin with the teacher reading aloud an enjoyable story or text aloud to students. Then, each student will select a book from the book basket nearby to read independently for an extended amount of time, usually no more than 20 minutes. During this time, the teacher will have individual conferences with designated students. Together, they will discuss the book, and the teacher will be able to evaluate the student's growth in reading. At the end of the block, several students will share what they read and whether they liked the books, just as adults share information with their friends about the books they're reading.

Writing Block

During this block, students will learn to think about and use their knowledge of phonics to write. Along with applying phonics, they will have an opportunity to practice handwriting and to learn about the writing process, grammar, and the mechanics of good writing.

Every day, the teacher will model writing during the mini-lesson. Then, all students will write their own pieces. On certain days, students will work individually with the teacher to learn to correct their errors, and they will publish their work as a book to be enjoyed by other classmates. At the end of the writing time each day, a few students will share their work with the class. It's truly surprising what an impact this block has on reading! Sometimes, the first text a student learns how to read is his or her own writing.

Working with Words Block

Students begin this block each day by studying words from the Word Wall. These words will be displayed on our wall all year for students to use as a resource. They are high-frequency words—grade-level words used frequently in reading and writing—that we expect students to spell correctly in their writing. We will use movements, such as clapping, snapping, and cheering, to learn to spell the words. We have a number of other activities to interest students during this word-exploration time. The second activity (Making Words, Guess the Covered Word, Rounding Up the Rhymes, etc.) allows students to explore words, word families (patterns), spellings, and phonics. It helps them see how they can use what they learn about words in their reading and writing.

Allington, R.L. (1983). The reading instruction provided readers of differing reading ability. *Elementary School Journal, 83,* 549–559.

Allington, R.L. (1991). Effective literacy instruction for at-risk children. M. Knapp & P. Shields (Eds.), *Better schooling for the children of poverty: Alternatives to conventional wisdom.* (p. 9–30). Berkeley, CA: McCutchan.

Anderson, R.C., Hiebert, E.H., Scott, J.A., & Wilkinson, I.A.G. (1985). *Becoming a nation of readers: The report of the commission on reading.* Washington, DC: U.S. Dept. of Education.

Bond, G.L., & Dykstra, R. (1967). The cooperative research program in first-grade reading instruction. *Reading Research Quarterly, 2,* 5–142. Reprinted in 1997 in Reading Research Quarterly, 32(4), 348–427.

Bryant, P.E., Bradley, L., MacLean, M., & Crossland, J. (1989). Nursery rhymes, phonological skills, and reading. *Journal of Child Language, 16(2),* 407–428.

Calkins, L.M. (1998). *The art of teaching writing* (2nd ed.). Portsmouth, N.H.: Heinemann.

Carr, E., & Ogle, D. (1987). KWL plus: a strategy for comprehension and summarization. *Journal of Reading, 30(7),* 626–631.

Cunningham, A.E., & Stanovich, K.E. (1998). What reading does for the mind. *American Educator, 22(1–2),* 8–15.

Cunningham, P.M. (2005). *Phonics they use: Words for reading and writing.* (4th ed.). NY: HarperCollins.

Cunningham, P.M., & Allington, R.L. (1999). *Classrooms that work: They can all read and write.* (2nd ed.). NY: Longman.

Cunningham, P.M., & Hall, D.P. (2008). *Making words for grade 2.* Boston: Allyn and Bacon.

Cunningham, P.M., & Hall, D.P. (1996a). *Building blocks: A framework for reading and writing in kindergartens that work.* Clemmons, NC: Windward.

Cunningham, P.M., & Hall, D.P. (1996b, 1999). *The four blocks: A framework for reading and writing in classrooms that work.* Clemmons, NC: Windward.

Professional References

Cunningham, P.M., & Hall, D.P. (2008). *Month-by-month phonics for second grade*. Greensboro, NC: Carson-Dellosa Publishing.

Cunningham, P.M., Hall, D.P., & Defee, M. (1991). Nonability grouped, multilevel instruction: A year in a first-grade classroom. *The Reading Teacher, 44,* 566–571.

Cunningham, P.M., Hall, D.P., & Defee, M. (1998). Nonability grouped, multilevel instruction: Eight years later. *The Reading Teacher, 51(8),* 652–664.

Duke, N.K., & Pearson, P.D. (2002). Effective practices for developing reading comprehension. A.E. Farstrup and S.J. Samuels (Eds.), *What research has to say about reading instruction* (3rd ed.) p. 205–242. Newark, DE: International Reading Association.

Graham, S., Harris, K.R., & Fink, B. (2000). Is handwriting causally related to learning to write?: Treatment of handwriting problems in beginning writers. *Journal of Educational Psychology, 92(4),* 620–633.

Graves, D.H. (1994). *A fresh look at writing*. Portsmouth, NH: Heinemann.

Hall, D.P., Prevatte, C., & Cunningham, P.M. (1995). Eliminating ability grouping and reducing failure in the primary grades. R.L. Allington & S. Walmsley (Eds.), *No quick fix: Rethinking literacy programs in America's elementary schools* (p. 137–158). NY: Teachers College Press.

Hillocks, G., Jr. (1986) *Research on written composition: New directions for teaching*. Urbana, IL: National Conference on Research in English/ERIC Clearinghouse on Reading and Communication Skills.

Hoffman, J., Roser, N.L., & Battle, J. (1993). Reading aloud in classrooms: From the modal to a "model." *The Reading Teacher, 46(6),* 496–505.

Johns, J.L. *Basic reading inventory* (5th ed.). (1994). Dubuque, IA: Kendall Hunt.

Langenberg, D.N. (Ed.) (2000). *Report of the National Reading Panel: Teaching children to read*. Washington, DC: U.S. Department of Health and Human Services.

National Reading Panel. (2000). *Teaching children to read: An evidence-based assessment of the scientific research literature on reading and its implications for reading instruction: Reports of the subgroups (National Institutes of Health Publication No. 00-4754)*. Washington, DC: National Institute of Child Health and Human Development.

Ogle, D. (1986). KWL: A teaching model that develops active reading of expository text. *The Reading Teacher, 39(6)*, 564-570.

Perfetti, C.A. (2003). The universal grammar of reading. *Scientific Studies of Reading, 7(1)*, 3–24.

Routman, R. (1995). *Invitations: Changing as teachers and learners, K-12* (2nd ed.). Portsmouth, NH: Heinemann.

Samuels, S.J. (2002). Reading fluency: Its development and assessment. A.E. Farstrup and S.J. Samuels (Eds.), *What research has to say about reading instruction* (3rd ed.) (p. 166–183). Newark, DE: International Reading Association.

Topping, K., and Paul, T. (1999). *Computer-assisted assessment of practice at reading: A large scale survey using Accelerated Reader data.* Reading and Writing Quarterly, 15, 213–231.

Veatch, J. (1959). *Individualizing your reading program: Self-selection in action.* NY: Putnam.

Young, S. (1994). *Scholastic rhyming dictionary.* NY: Scholastic.

Children's Books

Apperley, D. (2001). *Flip and flop.* New York, NY: Orchard Books.

Beaumont, K. (2005). *I ain't gonna paint no more!* Orlando, FL: Harcourt.

Cisco, C. (1997). *The lion and the mouse.* New York, NY: Sadlier-Oxford.

Cleary, B. (1965). *The mouse and the motorcycle.* New York, NY: HarperCollins.

Cowley, J. (1999). *Mrs. Wishy-Washy.* New Zealand: Shortland Publications.

dePaola, T. (1975). *Strega nona.* New York, NY: Simon & Schuster.

Dorros, A. (1991). *Animal tracks.* New York, NY: Scholastic.

Fox, M. (1992). *Hattie and the fox.* New York, NY: Simon & Schuster.

Gibbons, G. (1998a). *Cats.* New York, NY: Holiday House.

Gibbons, G. (1999). *Penguins!* New York, NY: Holiday House.

Gibbons, G. (1998b). *Sea turtles.* New York, NY: Holiday House.

Gibbons, G. (1993). *Sharks.* New York, NY: Holiday House.

Gibbons, G. (1995). *Wolves.* New York, NY: Holiday House.

Glaser, L. (1992). *Wonderful worms.* Brookfield, CT: Millbrook Press.

Jacquet, L. (2006). *March of the penguins.* Washington, DC: National Geographic Children's Books.

Lester, H. (1998). *Tacky in trouble.* Boston, MA: Houghton Mifflin.

Lester, H. (1988). *Tacky the penguin.* Boston, MA: Houghton Mifflin.

Lester, H. (1994). *Three cheers for Tacky.* Boston, MA: Houghton Mifflin.

Lionni, L. (1973). *Swimmy.* New York, NY: Knopf.

Martin, Jr., B. (1967). *Brown bear, brown bear, what do you see?* New York, NY: Holt, Rinehart and Winston.

McCloskey, R. (1976). *Make way for ducklings.* New York, NY: Viking.

Petersen, D. (1999). *Antarctica.* New York, NY: Children's Press.

Waber, B. (1979). *Ira sleeps over.* Boston, MA: Houghton Mifflin.

Williams, S. (1990). *I went walking.* San Diego, CA: Harcourt Brace Jovanovich.

Wood, A. J. (2002). *The little penguin.* New York, NY: Dutton Children's Books.

INDEX

(CONTINUED)

Mini-Lessons

N–P

Q-R

INDEX